Distant Waters

Contents

Foreword by Nick Lyons
6

Introduction by R. Valentine Atkinson
8

Dances with Trout – Alaska
John Gierach
10

Sterling Silver – Florida Keys
Russell Chatham
26

The Chalkstream Idyll – England
Neil Patterson
40

A Night at the Black Falls – Norway
Mike Fitzgerald
56

La Fiebre de las Bocas – Argentina
Ernest Schwiebert
70

Mornings – The Rocky Mountains
Nick Lyons
88

The Miramichi River – Canada
Leonard M. Wright, Jr.
104

Trout Among the Shadows – New Zealand
Verlyn Klinkenborg
118

Jingle Bones – Christmas Island
Peter Kaminsky
130

Fly-fishing in the Middle Ages – Russia
David Profumo
146

Sons – Mexico
Tom McGuane
160

My Platform of Despair – Iceland
Art Lee
176

Acknowledgments
192

Foreword

Two men, small against a vast Christmas Island flat. A man closer to the foreground, larger, leaning toward his prey. A man with fly rod in one hand, bonefish in the other, smiling broadly. A rod arced sharply to the pull of a New Zealand trout, the man just off dead center in the photograph. A scene through a frame of trees into the still, old, delicate world of a weedy Hampshire chalkstream with slick glides, a swan, men looking at the river, comparing notes, and a man hunkered in the shore grasses, his rod high and bent, and then a perfectly huge brown trout, held out for appreciation. The fecund world of a Montana trout stream, with snow-peaks in the distance, the rumpling of the surface that is a good trout's rise, and then another huge trout held forth. These are not only glimpses into a fly-fisher's distant waters but events – archetypical dramas. This is Val's world.

Iceland to Christmas Island, Alaska to the Keys to Norway, Argentina, Russia, Mexico, England, New Zealand, Canada, Montana – wherever there are wilder coasts, or intimate riverbanks where fly-fishermen travel to pursue their sport, Val Atkinson has traveled, with his eager, extraordinary eye and camera. Since the late 1960's when he quit being an art director in an advertising agency in Columbus, Ohio, he has been traveling with fly rod and camera, at first photographing in stark and memorable black and white. I especially remember his early shot of a partial, extended arm holding a curved fly rod, the long line connected to an outsize fish funneling just under the surface, mad to escape. I get shivers whenever I see it. Then, more than a decade later, his color photographs began to appear - stunning, brilliantly conceived and framed images that etch into our brains those distant waters where fly-fishing happens.

Though many of those waters are here enlivened with the words of Verlyn Klinkenborg, Thomas McGuane, John Gierach, and a host of other fine writers, for me Val's remarkable photographs are the heart of this rare book. He captures, better than any photographer working today, the character of unique places, the faces and body attitudes of those engaged in fly-fishing, the happy thingness of equipment.

It is winter, in a gray city, as I write this, and I am delighted to have the broad panorama of the fly-fishing experience spread out before me. It brightens my spirit, reminds me of other distant waters I know or dream of fishing. I cannot think of anyone who fly-fishes, anywhere, who will not love Val's photos. He gives us the fly-fisher's world.

Nick Lyons

Introduction

I caught my first trout on a fly rod at the age of seven. That hatchery fish from the Wissahickon Park outside Philadelphia sparked a flame that still keeps me warm.

Twenty years ago I started taking my camera on fishing trips, after realizing that there was a lot more to angling than catching fish. Over the years I have learned to combine these two passions into my life's work.

This book fulfills a dream of enabling me to share these passions with you. For the last ten years, I've been traveling around the world to some very special places and I can honestly say that I've enjoyed each one more than the last.

I must confess that in recent years the challenge of making a really great picture has often outweighed the desire to catch a fish. However, fly-fishing and photography go very well together. The trick is knowing just when to put down the rod and pick up the camera.

Some years ago I defined my sense of enjoyment in a poem:

> *Happiness for me is a dusty, lonely road in summer with a full tank*
> *of gas and a trunk full of fishing tackle*
> *Escaping the crowds of the city for the wonderful solitude of*
> *the river and its inhabitants;*
> *To breathe crisp, clean air and to feel the sun*
> *on your back as you wade the river.*

These days I travel farther afield, but it's the same need for beauty and solitude that motivates me. In the following pages you'll see some of the places where I found it. It is my sincere desire that these images share with you the passion for these wild and romantic places. If they do, then hopefully, you will also share the desire to cherish, respect, and protect what wilderness remains in this world, and actively to resist the greed which flourishes and threatens. Our success would help to realize another dream of mine – that you and your grandchildren will also see these places one day, and find them as lovely and pristine as they appear here.

Here's to truth, adventure, and passion.

There are several people whom I should like to thank, starting with my parents, who, though not fishers themselves, instilled in me the ethic that fishing was "all-American" as eating apple pie, and often remarked that I would rather fish than eat.

I would like to express my heartfelt gratitude, too, to my friend and partner, Susan Rockrise, who urged me to new heights in everything. She taught me much about respect; and how, through faith and courage, to pursue what I believed in and wanted. She is a truly remarkable human being.

My sincerest appreciation also goes to Frontiers International Travel – unquestionably the finest sporting travel agency in the world today. I've been their staff photographer since 1986 and have gone to all the destinations in this book on assignments for them. They have changed my life. Thank you for letting me be a part of your family.

I should like to thank all of the world-class writers whose stories appear in this book. Thank you for your generosity.

And lastly, I should like to thank all of my fishing friends throughout the US and the world for your friendship and continued support, including Alex Mitchell and Nick Zoll, who have helped and encouraged with this book.

R. Valentine Atkinson

Dances with Trout

Alaska

JOHN GIERACH

"Most days we spent two or three hours flying over genuinely trackless country, often at altitudes of two hundred feet or less, which is low enough to see bears, caribou, and even tundra swans clearly, not to mention stream after stream running red from spawning sockeye salmon. I must have asked a dozen people why the salmon turn red in the rivers, and the only one who knew was a native guy. 'It's so the bears can see 'em,' he said."

The backcountry of Alaska is a perfect silence broken by the sound of motors: generators, outboards and especially the droning of float planes. Up there the single-engine plane is the equivalent of the pickup truck. Once you're away from the state's handful of roads – in the bush where the fishing is really good – a plane is your only way of getting anywhere, not to mention getting back.

I was in Alaska not too long ago with my friends DeWitt Daggett and Dan Heiner. DeWitt is a publisher and Dan is the managing field editor of an outdoor magazine (which means he manages to get into the field as much as possible).

We fished from three different lodges – technically, two lodges and a hotel – and spent a lot of time in the air, which is standard procedure. There would be the flight in and then, most days, weather permitting, we'd fly out to this or that river in the morning to be left with a guide and maybe an inflatable raft or a boat stashed on site. Then we'd be picked up at a predetermined place and time to be flown back to the lodge in the evening. Or what passes for evening. In the Alaskan summer there's a little bit of duskiness in the wee hours, but nothing those of us from "down below," as they say, would call night.

Most days we spent two or three hours flying over genuinely trackless country, often at altitudes of 200 feet or less, which is low enough to see bears, moose, caribou, and even tundra swans clearly, not to mention stream after stream running red from spawning

ABOVE *Early-morning activity centers around the dock at Bristol Bay, where planes and boats prepare for the day's fishing.*

sockeye salmon. I must have asked a dozen people why the salmon turn red in the rivers, and the only one who knew was a native guy. "It's so the bears can see 'em," he said.

We often had the rivers we'd chosen entirely to ourselves, and that sense of loneliness was enhanced by the knowledge that now and then the plane doesn't show up to take you back to the nice, cozy lodge. This doesn't happen often (it never happened to us) but there is weather to consider, or engine trouble, and every now and then a pilot will get sick or even just forget that he was supposed to pick you up, only to slap his forehead in a bar two days later, turn to the guy on the next stool, and say, "Oh, shit." Fishermen are seldom lost for ever, but they've been known to get stranded for a while.

At the time it seemed like an outrageous odyssey, but back in Anchorage I found that we'd only gone a couple of inches down the Alaska Peninsula on a map

of the state that would cover the average kitchen table. I went out on the front porch and tried to extrapolate the feeling of vastness from our own little trip to all the rest of that game- and fish-infested, largely roadless open land as an exercise in meditation. I sat there through two cans of beer and couldn't do it, but I did remember something Wallace Stegner had said on an audio-tape DeWitt's company produced – something about how you don't even have to go into the wilderness to get its benefits, just knowing it's out there is a great comfort.

ABOVE *Twilight falls on Nonvianuk Lake in Katmai National Park. This is as dark as it gets in mid-summer. The sound of loons calling echoes across the waters in the dusk.*

When we boarded the Alaska Airlines flight from Anchorage to Iliamna, the stewardess got on the intercom and said, "Fasten your seat belts and, yes, the reds are running." That was welcome news because I was psyched to catch salmon, as was everyone else on the plane. There were sixty-something passengers and exactly that many rod cases. No briefcases, no lap-top computers. We were there in late

ABOVE *Some popular Alaskan flies. The colorful patters are for salmon. The deer hair mice are for rainbows. Note the eyes and ears on the mice.*

July so any salmon caught would probably be sockeyes, aka "reds." These are a marginal fly rod fish, many people said, but that hardly mattered.

For one thing, I'd spent a week fishing for Atlantic salmon in Scotland that same summer and had gotten skunked. I wasn't exactly looking for revenge (although going after, but not catching, a certain kind of fish does give you a long-lasting itch), there was just the idea of those millions of big fish that live some-where out at sea and then run up into the rivers once a year, past orcas, and seals, and bears, to spawn and then die. When you come from a place where there are fewer fish and they pretty much stay put, that's romantic stuff.

I got into salmon on our first day on the water. We'd flown into the mouth of the Tazamina River and then motored upstream a mile or so. The water was full of sockeyes, but that didn't seem to interest anyone much except me. Dan, DeWitt, and the guide were calmly speculating on where the rainbows and grayling might be, while I kept leaning over the gunnels saying, "Jesus Christ, look at all the salmon. Stop the god damn boat!" Most of the fish were nice and silvery, still fresh from the sea.

When we finally beached on a sand bar the guide got the other two guys going with streamers and then led me to a huge pod of sockeyes. He told me to rig a pink Polar Shrimp with split shot, as if I were fishing for trout with a nymph. One thing about the Alaskans: unlike the Scots, they fish for salmon as if they actually want to catch them, with sink-tip lines and lead.

When the guide saw that I was rigging up an old Payne nine-and-a-half-foot light salmon rod with a brand-new Peerless #6 reel, he said he'd never seen one of those and asked to try it.

"Shoot," he said, "this is a little heavy, but it casts real nice."

There were fifty salmon in a pool not ten feet from where I was standing. "I'm glad you like the rod," I said, "but give it back."

I had a fish on for a minute or two and lost him. Then I got a good hookup, but the fish was snagged in the back. It weighed six or seven pounds and took longer to land than it should have.

I thought, yeah, I've heard about this. There are those who say the plankton-eating sockeyes don't take flies and the best you can do is foul hook them, and there are others who say they do too take flies if you do it right. The rules say the fish is a keeper if it's hooked somewhere in the face, ahead of the gill covers.

If I remember right, I landed seven salmon that afternoon, four of which were hooked in or so close to the mouth that I'd say they either ate or tried to eat the fly.

And that's as far as I care to delve into that controversy. I will say that when a sockeye is hooked near the front it fights real good, especially on a bamboo rod.

Those first few days we fished from the Iliaska Lodge owned by Ted and Mary Gerkin. There's a long story here, and if you'd like to hear it you should read Ted's book, *Gamble at Iliamna*, because he tells it much better than I could. Anyway, it was here that I began to understand how sockeye salmon were viewed by Alaskan fly-fishers.

The sockeyes, along with the kings, silvers, chums, and pinks, form the basis for the entire ecology of these watersheds. The number of fish in these runs is astonishing: six million in this drainage, nineteen million in that one, and there are hundreds of drainages.

Salmon often run all the way up into the smaller rivers and creeks, many of which are connected by large lakes. There are resident grayling and some Dolly Vardens in these streams, but the big rainbow trout and Arctic char are only in the flowing water in significant numbers when they follow the salmon runs up out of the lakes. Sometimes a fisherman will say that Such-and-Such River isn't good for big rainbows yet because the salmon aren't in. If you're new at this you'll have to ask him what the hell he's talking about.

The trout, char, and grayling feed on salmon eggs that are dribbled by the ripe hen salmon as they run up the rivers and then later on the ones that wash out of the spawning reeds. This sounds like an incidental dietary footnote until you multiply the salmon by millions and get tons of protein from stray eggs alone.

BELOW *An Orange Comet.*

The fish are really onto these things. It's said that big rainbows will swim over and nudge ripe hen salmon to dislodge eggs. Every guide and bush pilot I talked to claims to have seen that.

Still later, after the spawn when the salmon all die, these same gamefish feed on bits of rotted salmon meat dislodged by the current. It's hard to picture, but in this scheme the pretty rainbow trout, char and grayling fall into the same ecological niche as maggots and vultures.

The standard flies are salmon-egg patterns and sickly beige-colored "flesh flies," tied from rabbit fur. Naturally, these are fished on a dead drift. This may not be what you'd call classy stuff, but it does match the hatch perfectly.

The dying and dead salmon are also eaten by gulls, ravens, eagles, otters, and so on, not to mention aquatic insects, which then go on to feed the salmon parr and smolts before they return to the sea, as well as the grayling, trout, char and such during those times when there are no salmon in the rivers. Then the young salmon themselves form part of the diet for other gamefish. In the middle of all this, you can go to the places where rivers enter lakes and fish streamers for big char collected there to feed on migrating smolts. The schools of char are often under flocks of excited, hungry gulls and terns.

That's the obvious stuff you can see from a boat or while wading a river. There's also the plankton/salmon/seal/orca connection out at sea. In the grand scheme, that's what salmon do: they bring the nutrients from the ocean far up into the freshwater rivers, lakes, and streams and there's no way I can convey the magnitude of it. It's just something you have to see.

ABOVE *A Bead-eye Salmon Bugger.*

BELOW *An Orange Flash.*

And then there are the bears. Alaskan brown bears – along with rainbow trout – put on a large part of every year's growth gorging on salmon, and once you've stepped in a huge, steaming pile of bear crap you begin to see that their droppings are not an insignificant contribution to the fertilizer needed to grow the grasses that are fed upon by the caribou that are now and then eaten by the bears – and so on.

This is efficient, economical, messy, smelly, mystically circular, and temperamental. It's especially temperamental if you count the commercial netting of salmon – the "nylon curtain," they call it – that can screw things up seriously when it's not properly regulated, as most people will tell you it, in fact, is not. Take away

ABOVE *Susan Rockrise caught 79 salmon during her week at Bristol Bay Lodge in southwestern Alaska. She is shown here with one of them.*

ABOVE *A beautiful wilderness setting for an overnight camp.*

the salmon, as some would gladly do for a single year's profit, and the ecosystem would die.

They say that the silvers and, in some circumstances, the kings are the real fly rod salmon in Alaska. The sockeyes are loved as a food fish and for their overall contribution to the food chain, but in the circles we were traveling in – fly-fishers and fly-fishing guides – they don't seem to be too highly rated.

One morning at Iliaska when the weather was too shocked in for flying, some of the guides drove a crew of us over to the Newhalen River to join 75 or so other fishermen who were dredging for sockeyes. This is called "combat zone fishing," and one of the guides told me the Newhalen was nothing. "You should see the rivers you can drive to from Anchorage," he said.

I got into it after a while, even though I claim not to like fishing in a crowd or chunking lead. I mean, what the hell: these were big fish and this was Alaska, where things are sometimes done differently. In the true spirit of things, I got deeply interested in killing some fish to take home.

By the way, I believe that "chunking" is the proper, common term. It's onomatopoeic, coming from the distinctive "chunk" sound split shot makes when it hits the water.

When the ceiling lifted after a few hours, Ted and another pilot flew over to pick us up and take us to a secluded little river to catch big rainbow trout, possibly on dry flies. "You're about to go from the ridiculous to the sublime," Ted said.

Rainbows are what the guides and lodge owners brag about most – in terms of both numbers and size – and they're what many visiting fly-fishers are looking for. After all, this is one of the few places on earth where, at the right time, with some skill, a little luck and maybe the right guide, you can bag your ten- or twelve- or (if the stories can be believed) even your fifteen-pound rainbow on a fly rod. The fish will be scavenging behind a run of salmon instead of sipping mayflies but, if you connect, it will be a by-God, double-digit wallhanger.

Not far from Iliamna Lake by float plane, on a river the name of which I've been asked not to mention, I landed a six-pound rainbow on a dry fly. It was a nice fish, big enough to make the lodge book (volume III), in which, among other things, you can record for posterity any trout over four pounds caught on a dry.

It was a nice fish, but not a great one by Alaskan standards; memorable only because it was hooked on a floating caddis pattern instead of on a sunken salmon egg, flesh fly or streamer. On the other hand, it was probably the biggest trout I've ever caught on a dry fly.

People have written pages in that lodge book about a single, good fish – eloquent stories filled with keen observations and humour – but I couldn't think of anything more profound than, "Six-pound rainbow on a #14 olive Stimulator," dated and signed. It's not that I wasn't happy, I was just a little tongue-tied.

We caught salmon on wet flies and split shot, nice-sized Arctic char on eggs and Woolly Bugger streamers, rainbows on streamers and eggs, and one day I got into some pretty Dolly Vardens, once again on eggs. Apparently, you don't do a lot of dry fly-fishing in Alaska and I understand some fishermen on their first trip there are a little disillusioned by that.

I won't say I was actually disappointed, but there were a few times when I got

ABOVE *A Muddler Minnow.*

ABOVE *The weather can change rapidly in Alaska. This morning was sunny and virtually cloudless. Within twenty minutes of my admiring its beauty and taking this photograph, the sky had been overcome by dark clouds and I was watching the pouring rain.*

enough of lead and sink-tips and flies that looked less like bugs and more like bangles from a stripper's costume. And, yes, those did happen to be the few times when we weren't catching fish. I've noticed that certain fishing tactics seem a lot more acceptable when they're working.

Still, that day on the river that Ted Gerkin asked me not to write about – the one where the big rainbows would come up to a dry caddis fly – was a tremendous relief, and so was our first afternoon at Wood River Lodge on the Agulawok River.

There were fish rising in front of the cabin as we lugged our gear from the plane, and when we rushed down there we found that they were rainbows and grayling, both up to eighteen or twenty inches, rising to a this-and-that hatch of caddis, mayflies and small stoneflies. The fish weren't too picky, but we did have to fish flies that at least approximated the appearance of the real bugs. I was already in the water with my five-weight rod strung up, DeWitt was playing a fish and Dan had just missed a strike, when I learned that I had to run back to the cabin and dig my dry-fly boxes out of the bottom of the duffel bag. At that point in the trip I had caught countless big fish, but it almost killed me that, for five minutes, Dan and DeWitt were getting them while I was looking for those damned fly boxes.

The next day we could have flown out once again to catch great big something-or-others someplace else, but we unanimously voted to stay and fish the river right in front of the lodge. They gave us two guides with boats, and we fished from right after breakfast – say, eight in the morning – until dusk, which would have been going on midnight. Sure, we broke for a shore lunch and dinner at the lodge, but that's still a long day. In fact, this has happened to me at least once every time I've gone north. I say, "Jeeze, I'm kind of tired for some reason," and the bright-eyed guide says, "Well, we have been fishing for about sixteen hours now."

We caught rainbows, some nice big Arctic char, and my biggest sockeye of the trip (ten pounds) on streamers, but what I remember most clearly now are the grayling.

They were almost all good-sized, maybe fifteen to twenty inches, and throughout the day we'd find pods of them rising in the slack water beside faster currents. "That's because they're a lazy fish," Duncan said. That's Duncan Oswald, one of several guides at Wood River who specialize in fly-fishing. He also ties the flies for the lodge and knows the river's hatches. That's significant because in Alaska you don't have to know the hatches to catch fish.

I fished for the grayling with a seven-foot, nine-inch Mike Clark bamboo rod and Dan broke out a sweet little Pezon & Michelle Parabolic. Neither rod raised any eyebrows and, in fact, I was surprised at how many cane rods I saw on that trip.

Apparently, many Alaskan fly-fishers have a darling little bamboo stashed away for just these kinds of occasions.

As I said, the hatches were scattered, but the best was a fall of size fourteen dark stoneflies. The grayling would execute a refusal rise to a #14 Royal Wulff, sometimes eat an Elk Hair Caddis, Irresistible or Stimulator, and absolutely hammer an elegantly simple deer hair and calf tail stonefly of Duncan's own design. I brought a few of these home with me to copy.

Some people will tell you that grayling are easy fish – the bluegills of the north – but I've never found them to be like that. The few times I've fished for them in their native range, they've been catchable, but far from pushovers: easy enough that you can usually get some, but still hard enough that each fish is an event. And, of course, they're unbelievably, iridescently beautiful. The perfect gamefish, in other words.

That night at the lodge over gin and tonics, one of the other guides said it was too bad we hadn't gone off with him to catch the "pigs" but, more for Duncan's benefit than ours, I think, he said he did realize that a salmon egg is "chunked," while a dry fly is "presented."

We saw lots of bears in Alaska. They were following the salmon runs, as we were – inadvertently or otherwise – so it was unavoidable. These animals are called Alaskan brown bears, although there's some disagreement among the scientists about whether they're a separate species from the grizzly. The main difference is size. A big brown bear looks just like a grizzly, but stands a foot taller and weighs as much as 600 pounds more. When you're sharing a gravel bar with one, size does seem to be the defining factor.

A big sow and a yearling cub came down to the Newhalen River the first day we fished it. I was about fourth in the line of fishermen upstream from the spot the bears wanted. When one of the guides hooted "Bear!" I looked, broke off the eight-pound salmon I was playing without a second thought and began wading slowly but deliberately upstream, as they tell you to do. Dan, who doesn't like bears much, was just ahead of me. He didn't say anything, but he was making a quiet noise deep in his throat that sounded like the cooing of a pigeon.

Later, DeWitt said it was interesting to see the "ripple of recognition" go through us when the bears waded out into the river.

We saw bears almost everyday, and there are three things people tell you about them: that, nine times out of ten, the bear will decline a confrontation; that if he doesn't decline, it's probably your fault; and that a bear's personal space is no less than fifty yards. That seemed awfully close. I found that I had to be at about 200 before it would occur to me that the adults were handsome and the cubs were actually pretty cute. Bears scare me badly, but I still like them a lot, which I take as evidence that I've negotiated something heavy.

We had only a couple of ticklish bear encounters, one of which we had in a spot where a small creek entered a lake. The plan was to wade up the creek a half mile or so to a place where, we'd been assured, there were huge rainbows and grayling, but there was a sow and two cubs around the first bend, so we had to turn back and work the inlet, where there didn't seem to be too many fish.

I won't try to describe the whole, grim dance in detail, but eventually a young male bear came down to the inlet and made it known that we had blundered into his personal space and that he wasn't pleased. Since he was on shore and we were

BELOW *A father and son, together with their guide, proudly display yet another bright silver salmon, fresh from the sea.*

BELOW *Early morning coffee in the camp, and a toast to another great day in paradise.*

RIGHT *Brown bears fishing for salmon at Brooks Falls in Katmai National Park. From the safety of an elevated wooden platform, anglers and tourists can watch as many as a dozen bears catch dinner.*

already up to our armpits in the lake, we had a little trouble getting out of his way, although we tried. At one point the bear gave us some negative body language – lowered head, flattened ears. This doesn't sound like much on paper, but on site it's pretty damned impressive.

Throughout the whole thing our guide, Nanci Morris, spoke in a charming voice, first to the bear, then to us, and she never unholstered her Smith and Wesson .44 Magnum. She was the picture of composure and said later she was more worried about that sow getting nervous because boars are known to attack cubs.

It turned out okay, but I was glad to hear the deep, unmistakable drone of the DeHavilland Beaver Nanci calls the Cream Puff coming to pick us up. It occurred to me that having an airplane come and save you from a bear is a great way to get over your fear of flying. When the plane taxied in, Dan waded out and kissed a pontoon, able to kid around now because it seemed we'd live.

Nanci is the head guide (excuse me, "Director of Sportfishing") at the Quinnat Landing Hotel in the town of King Salmon. Her specialty is trophy-sized kings, and in some magazine article or brochure she was once dubbed "the queen of the king salmon guides." Naturally, that stuck, as embarrassing publicity always does.

When I said something about getting to be head guide at a place like that at an obviously tender age, Nanci said, "Yeah, and, not to put too fine a point on it, try doing it as a woman."

I could see that. Competence is admired in a place like King Salmon, but men

far outnumber women and at times the horniness is almost palpable. And it's a little rough – in a pleasant way for a tourist, but rough nonetheless. Over some beers in the hotel bar a pilot named Red told me, "We try to make a year's living here in five or six months, so we fight sleep deprivation half the year and depression the other half." He also said, gazing wistfully out at the Naknik River, "Ah, Alaska. She seduces you every summer and then abandons you every winter."

Anyway, Nanci does seem to love that plane with something close to a passion. As head guide, she almost always manages to schedule it for her own trips and, although she talked about other things in the two days we all spent together, she kept coming back to the Cream Puff. When we walked down to the dock to board it or when it banked in to land and pick us up, she'd say, "Just look at it. God!"

The first time I saw the Cream Puff it was sitting at a dock on the Naknik River and we were sitting in the bar at Quinnat Landing, near the big picture windows, eating thick steaks and talking about the fishing. During a lull in the conversation, Nanci gazed out at the Beaver and said, "See that plane out there? I love that plane. If that plane was a man, I just might say 'I do.'"

At which point every man in the joint looked out the window at the lovely old purple Beaver. Its big radial engine was idling. At that range it sounded like the purring of a large, happy cat.

ALASKA – FACTFILE

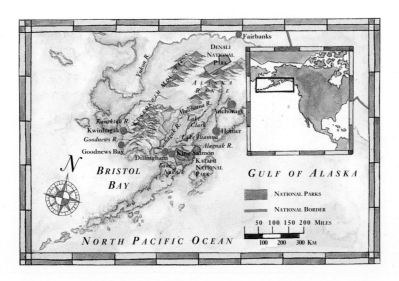

BACKGROUND

Alaska has come to signify wilderness. It became the 49th United State in 1959. Its lakes and rivers are famous for their abundance of fish, and especially their Pacific salmon. As a result, Alaskan fishing, spectacular for the fly-fisherman, is also the state's greatest source of economic wealth. The Iliamna Lake, featured in this chapter, is the second-largest freshwater lake in the United States. It drains into the Bristol Bay and the Bering Sea. Given its name by the Inuit, the lake has its own myth: lying at the bottom of the Iliamna is a giant blackfish, which bites the bottoms of canoes as they are paddled across the water!

WHEN TO GO

In spring, all fishing locations are affected by run-off from the melting snow. Not only will water levels be at their peak, but water temperatures will be fairly low, and if the temperature is lower than 45°F (8°C), salmon and rainbow trout usually won't go out of their way to take a fly.

By about the end of June, water levels will have dropped quite drastically, unless there has been an abnormal amount of rainfall. In the freestone streams, optimum insect activity will coincide with stabilizing water levels, and higher water temperatures. During this period nymph-fishing will continue to be productive, but as the juvenile insects mature, dry fly-fishing quickly becomes very fruitful.

Much of Alaska's rain comes in September and October before the snow falls. Previously stable water conditions can change vastly in a matter of several days. This is also the time when the salmon, especially the sockeyes, lay their eggs – more and more of the trout's, char's, and grayling's diet will be made up of this salmon roe.

Of the five species of Pacific salmon, the kings (or chinooks), which are the largest, are usually the first to appear, during the middle of June, and their run continues through the end of July. Kings are always found in the deepest parts of the river and strike gaudy streamers, fished deep with high-density lines. Chums and sockeyes follow the kings, usually appearing around the end of June, and run through the middle of July. Chums take the fly aggressively and are tough fighters; sockeyes are fussy about what they'll take, but their initial run is best compared to the blazing run of a large bonefish.

Silver salmon appear in the rivers around August 10 – earlier or later depending upon the river and its location. They run well into September. Silvers are a good fighting fish, averaging 10 to 12 lbs.

As well as the salmonoids, Alaska has huge and wild rainbow trout, which are available throughout the season, along with a vast array of other resident freshwater species including grayling, arctic char, lake trout, pike, and Dolly Varden.

THE FISHING

Alaskan fishing is affected by fish migrations, alterations in the weather, and the changing habits of freshwater fish species. To get the best out of these waters, it is vital for anglers to be versatile with their fishing methods. Combinations of rods, reels, and, most importantly, a selection of lines, enable a fisherman to change approaches quickly, and conform to a particular fish's preference.

Whether experts or beginners, all anglers tend to adapt quickly to Alaskan fishing techniques. Alaska is among the best destinations to learn about fly-fishing. Simply, fly-fishermen will encounter more big fish in Alaska in a single day than they ever thought possible. Virtually all of the fishing is done on moving rivers, with strong currents that add an excitement to the fight not found when fishing lakes.

THE TACKLE

RODS: There are two rods that are often used in Alaskan fishing waters: an 8 to 9 ft rod for a 6 or 7 wt line; and an 8½ to 9½ ft rod for an 8 or 9 wt line. A rod of the latter size is desirable for rainbows on bigger rivers, sockeye, and silver salmon fishing, or anywhere that you may need to stretch your cast with heavier lines.

You should select rods according to seasonal conditions and your personal style; for example, a lighter rod will be better suited to smaller creek and outlet fishing, which is common in June and July. In August and September a 7 and 8 wt rod combination may be better for rainbows in larger freestone streams and silver salmon (averaging 9 lbs plus) in broad rivers.

REELS: A top-quality reel is vital. Nearly all the fish that you catch should be played from the reel, so a good drag system is paramount. To complement a 6 or 7 wt rod, look for a reel and spare spools that will hold 150 yards of 20 lb backing with corresponding fly line. Pack a reel with capacity for 150 to 200 yards of 20 lb backing as well as your fly line for 8 or 9 wt rods. Drag strength and smoothness is crucial to playing and landing the biggest fish species.

LINES: A selection of lines is at the heart of a versatile fishing system for Alaska. Floating lines, floating sinking-tips, and sinking shooting heads allow fishermen to work flies in the correct depth range. Carry extra spools with you in your vest or tackle bag.

Pack a weight-forward floating line for your 6 or 7 wt rod as well as a 10 to 15 ft super-high density

sinking-tip line on an extra spool. Among your lines for your 8 or 9 ft rods you should also include a 10 to 15 ft super-high density sinking-tip.

LEADERS: Alaska's fish are generally not leader-shy. Your main consideration is a selection of leaders that will correctly turn over the array of fly patterns. Include both 6 ft and 7½ ft leaders with tippet sizes ranging from 5X (3 lbs) on the light side to 15 lbs on the heavy side.

Typically, 8 to 20 lb tippets are used for both salmon and trout/char/grayling. Also include extra tippet spools in those sizes. As a general rule, you will find shorter leaders more efficient with the sinking-tip and sinking lines, to keep the fly down deep with the line. In fact, it is a common practice among guides in Alaska to cut another foot or two off a leader as short as 6 ft, but remember to pay attention to tippet diameter so that the short leaders will swim the fly properly.

FLIES: In choosing flies you may find many patterns that work in the "lower 48" appropriate for Alaskan waters. The special Pacific salmon flies and salmon-related or egg flies are unique and effective patterns which may be familiar to steelheaders of the Northwest's and Great Lakes' drainages. By far the most-used fly in Alaska is the heavily weighted Black, Brown, or Olive Wooly Bugger tied in sizes 2 to 6.

All freshwater species feed on subaquatic insects, minnows, sculpins, smolt, and salmon eggs. In times of abundance, the salmon fry or eggs may be the major portion of the diet of these freshwater fish – select flies with this in mind.

Pacific salmon kings (chinooks), silvers (cohos), chums (dogs), sockeyes (reds), and pinks (humpies) do not feed once they enter fresh water. Consequently, salmon flies are primarily attractor patterns. These are designed to entice salmon to strike by using color or movement rather than imitating a food source. Many of these flies also work interchangeably for other freshwater species; typically, they are heavily weighted.

Some of the more successful dry flies are the Light Cahill, Royal, and Grizzly Wulffs; and Irresistibles, Humpies, and improved Stonefly or high-floating Caddis imitations.

Take a supply of your favorite dries that work on home waters. Many of the spent wing or soft hackle patterns that have been developed excel in Alaskan waters, and midging for trout, char, and grayling with tiny size 22 to 24's is a lot of fun here.

Bread and butter for Alaska's trout are all-purpose Dark Stoneflies, Wooly Worms, Bitch Creeks, Helgrammites, Leeches, and Montana Nymphs. Make sure that your wets are heavily weighted in sizes 4 to 8.

Streamers and bucktails that are good for salmon and trout are the Black Nose Dace, Alaska Mary Ann, Gray Ghost, Baby Rainbow Trout, Blue Smolt, Lefty's Deceiver, and Polar Chuck, which should be tied on long shank hooks in sizes 2 to 6; and Mickey Finns or any Red-and-White or Orange-and-White Bucktails. The Marabou Muddler and a selection of large sculpin patterns are also very effective trout and char flies.

ESSENTIAL TRAVEL EQUIPMENT

Alaska's weather can be very changeable, so take clothing that can be put on and taken off in layers. Pack a lightweight jacket, warm sweater, and wool trousers, a wool cap, and a raincoat. Don't forget insect repellent – the bugs can be utterly ruthless.

ABOVE *Silvers are among the most popular species of Pacific salmon. They take well and are strong fighters. Returning Pacific salmon have a vast range of breeding colors during their spawning runs. The males may develop a hooked jaw or kype.*

FLIES, CLOCKWISE FROM BOTTOM LEFT
An Orange Sockeye; a Red Girdle Bug; a Green Boss; a Matuka; an Olive Matuka; a Babine Special; an Eggsucking Leech; a Zonker Natural; a Brown Wooly Bugger; an Orange Super Comet; a Muddler; and an Orange Zonker.

Sterling Silver
Florida Keys

RUSSELL CHATHAM

"This is one of those spring mornings you always hope for; still, humid, and already warm, so that the guides at the Sea Center on Big Pine Key feel the air and call it a tarpon day. As you ease out of the cut, enormous clouds are stacked around the horizon, nacreous and pillowy. Later a breeze may rise out of the southwest, but now the water is slick as mercury, its pastel patina reflecting the tops of the tallest clouds."

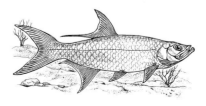

The elemental flatness of the Florida Keys is compelling and mysterious in its thin plane of reflective brilliance. Within their own horizontal galaxy, the flats are as inscrutable as the empyrean blue water of the Gulf Stream itself, far outside the shoals where you look down along sharp, beveled shafts of light that narrow into blackness thousands of feet above the ocean floor.

Inshore, and out of sight of the Atlantic's barrier reefs, among the very Keys themselves, the horizon is often lost somewhere behind refulgent bands of light and shimmering heat waves. On certain hot, humid days without wind, distant mangrove islands are seen only as extraneous tubes of gray-green, lying inexplicably in the silver atmosphere like alien spaceships.

Over in the backcountry, the Gulf side of the Keys, long plateaus of uneven coral stall the tide and agitate it so the waterscape vibrates and sparkles. The whole of this inside territory is an unfathomably complex tapestry of radical design.

Few people understand that this vast district is one of the great wildernesses of North America. Travelers, as they fly between Marathon Key or Key West and Miami, are temporarily enthralled by the complicated pattern of lime-green channels and basins, the ochre and light-sienna coral and sand flats, the islands. But almost no one ever goes there .

Most of those who do have occupational reasons: sponge, lobster and conch fishermen, shrimpers, and fishing guides. Groups of bird watchers sometimes visit certain special Keys. Skin divers occasionally go out and poke around old wrecks. And lastly, there are sportsmen.

Even within this last category is bracketed yet another minority within the minority: a fisherman who, in the opinion of some, carries it too far, bringing with him restyled nineteenth-century attitudes, seemingly inappropriate equipment and a full-on desire to proceed without secondary motives. Sometimes alone, sometimes with a close friend or

ABOVE *A collection of Fender Flies, Brook's Argentines, and Stu Apte's Flies. Hooks need to be extremely sharp to penetrate the tough, bony mouth of the tarpon.*

LEFT *Guinea-fowl feathers that have been dyed blue.*

ABOVE *A pod of tarpon schooled up in shallow water. These are small, ten- to twenty-pounders. They go on growing to weigh up to 200 pounds or more.*

perhaps a sympathetic hired guide, with benefit of only a small open skiff, a pole to push it, a fly rod and a perverse desire to be out of fashion, he goes out there to fish for tarpon.

It takes leisuretime and a nature disposed toward contemplation, and sometimes contradiction, to develop passion for pastimes with surface pointlessness. In the instance of fly-fishing for tarpon, a certain quantum of cash on hand is also required, although in no way is this an endeavor suited to the idle rich, or, for that matter, to anyone else slightly dotty. You need all your faculties.

Suppose you have the time, the money and the faculties. Assuming you want to expend them all on exotic fishing, why would you choose to go for tarpon rather than, say, marlin, a historically much more glamorous quarry? Enter your aforementioned contemplative, sometimes contradictory character.

If you think about distilling fishing down to angling, then further, to angling's diamond center, you can scarcely come to any conclusion other than this: as the time immediately preceding that point at which the fish actually becomes hooked grows more difficult, intense and all-absorbing, the quality of the fishing improves.

After that, you want the take to be hard to manage – fascinating in and of itself – and the ensuing struggle to be, above all, noble. Now, these moments may follow so closely upon one another they seem as one, yet there remains a hierarchy, however blurred. Then, way down there at the bottom of the list, is the dead fish on your hands.

To catch a marlin you must troll. Say the word over and over again to yourself, drawing it out as if it were spelled with lots of o's and l's. There may be nothing on earth, except perhaps an unsuccessful bridge club luncheon, quite so boring as trolling. Trol-l-l-l-ing. Several hours of it should be enough to dull your senses so that when the captain or mate or speed of the boat, or whatever it is, finally hooks a fish and you are faced with the appalling prospect of an hour in the fighting chair, you simply would rather have a beer.

On quite another hand, nowhere else in the spectrum of available angling can there be found a more profoundly thrilling prelude to the hooking of a fish than in the stalking of tarpon in shallow water. The fly rod ups the ante considerably, too. In short, it's at least twice as much trouble as any other tackle you could use.

On the flats, where you must see everything, the search becomes an alarmingly patient and suspenseful intrigue. This game calls for a blend of refined skills, those of the hunter as well as the fisherman. It is a process, an experience, to which few, if any, ever really become fully initiated.

This is one of those spring mornings you always hope for; still, humid and already warm, so that the guides at the Sea Center on Big Pine Key feel the air and call it a tarpon day. As you ease out of the cut, enormous clouds are stacked around the horizon, nacreous and pillowy. Later a breeze may rise out of the southwest, but now the water is slick as mercury, its pastel patina reflecting the tops of the tallest clouds.

You are two days into a series of spring tides. This means you will be able to fish places that have been neglected during the preceding weeks, when there was not enough of a flood to bring the tarpon in. The plan will be to stake certain corners, then later, pole out some other banks.

When you shut down at your first stop it is suddenly as still as an empty room. The pole is taken from its chocks and your companion begins moving you into a higher position. It is still early, the sun at too oblique an angle to give real visibility.

Already it is getting hot, the high humidity causing a haze to form. It is impossible to see anything of the bottom beyond a few yards and you wonder how your friend knows where to stake. He is looking for the corner, he says, but you can notice no variation whatsoever in the even carpet of turtle grass.

Shortly, he pushes the stake in and ties off. You get up on the casting deck. Fish will be coming up the bank on your right, then cutting across where you are staked.

LEFT *Billy Pate jumping a tarpon at Buchanon Bank off Islamorada in the Keys. I sat on a small wooden stepladder for two days waiting for this picture to happen. I was ready when the fish jumped once and threw the hook. I got one frame – this is it.*

RIGHT *A Stu Apte Tarpon Fly.*

You pull off enough line for a throw, make one, then coil the running line neatly at your feet. You hold the fly in your hand, leaving a loop of fly line in the water long enough for a false cast. Now you wait and look.

There is plenty of time to think about the short-comings of your fly-casting, the different ways you might blow the chance when it comes. Your feet start to ache and you shift them a little so that later when you look down to make sure the fly line is not tangled, you see you're standing on it. You cast and recoil it carefully.

"Rollers. Hundred yards."

You look with extra intensity at the indefinite sheen as if the harder you stare the more likely you are to see something. Then they glint in unison, closer, and are gone again. The first wave of fright settles into your abdomen.

They're coming just as we thought. This way. Up the bank. Where are they? Where are they! It's not too soon to false-cast. Get going. Oh no. No! They're right here. At the boat. Flushing.

ABOVE *To watch as a tarpon swims over and engulfs your fly, then feels the hook and goes screaming off deep into your backing, is guaranteed to get your heart pounding.*

The frightened fish are scooting away, back into the sheen. There are marl muds everywhere around the boat, and the boils the fish make as they depart seem to send a shiver beneath the skiff you can feel on the bottom of your feet. You wish you had your blanket and a bottle of Jergens Lotion.

Several other pods of tarpon work their way up the tide. Always, though, their trajectory takes them past the skiff out of range. In an hour the surge of fish seems to have passed, gone on to Loggerhead or wherever they were going. You decide to pull the stake and pole out the bank.

As your companion begins to pole, you wish the sun would climb higher, the haze dissipate. You offer to take the pole, and are turned down.

The drab grasses tilt in the slow current like a billion signposts gone wrong. Poling, you will be obliged to concern yourself with trigonometry; moving tide, moving boat, moving fish, degree of intercept.

Without notice, basins appear, deep and crisply emerald over their white sand bottoms. Sometimes there are barracuda arranged in them like dark lines of doom.

Small, tan sharks glide past the boat; rays, too, moving over the flat as the tide floods. The bank is 1,000 yards long. Somewhere on its easy slope there must be tarpon. You surge smoothly forward, transom first, that gentle sound being the only one you hear. 300, 400 yards. Nothing.

What a strange way to fish this is. You might be out here for eight hours, running the boat ten, maybe twenty miles, and you never lose sight of the bottom. A drastic change in depth, one that might mean fish instead of no fish, or an easy pass through a little green cut rather than a grounded skiff or sheared pin, is twelve inches. Coming down off a plane at thirty knots at the wrong moment can mean settling into the grass so you will have to get out and push the heavy skiff until the bottom slopes away enough to get back in and pole your way out of it. Down here they always tell you, if something goes wrong with the engine, just get out and walk home.

"Twelve o'clock. Way out." Quite far ahead, you see the chain of sparkles as tarpon roll, gulping air. Tarpon on the bank. 150 yards? A hundred? Can't let them get too close. Stay in front of the first fish. Are there two? Six? A dozen? Nothing. Sheen. Reflection. Haze. Useless glasses. Boat's closing. Fish coming on. Remember. Fly in hand. Ready. Loop of line trailing. Glance to see it's not back in the way of the pole. Fly line still coiled. Loose. Strain your eyes. Look. Wakes? They're colder gray. Light. And dark. Not warm, not tan like the bottom. Movement will tell. Long. They're long, cool gray. Temples pound. The glare, relentless. Sheen. No shapes. No gray. Another wake. Still farther out than you thought. Never mind. Roll the line. Think about it. Streamer gone, in the air. Back loop flat . . . not so tight! Slow down. There he is, within range, rolling, enormous scales catching the light. Your friend is urging, warning. Now! Wait out the back-cast. Don't dump it. Wait. Drift. Know the intercept. Correct. Don't change direction too much. Not too much drive. Ease the cast off. Strip hard. Get his eye. Strip. A wake. Water rushing, churning. A take! Stay balanced, feel the turn, the tension. Now strike. Again, to the side. Again. Don't look up. Watch the line clear itself. Tarpon's in the air. Eye level, upside down, twisting, rattling. Push slack.

ABOVE *Billy Pate catching a "rat," which he later releases. A "rat" is what he calls a tarpon under 100 pounds. Billy holds the world record at 188 pounds caught on 16-pound tippet. Anglers are now looking to break the 200-pound mark.*

Running. Too fast. Another jump. Gone.

Tarpon are not used as food. You would think there must be some way they might be prepared, but they just aren't eaten. Nor are they taken for other commercial reasons. Once there was a scheme to convert them to pet food or fertilizer, a plan fortunately abandoned. In any case, there is no price per pound for tarpon, and no diners sit fidgeting with their utensils while their tarpon are being broiled.

On the other side of the ledger, this has come to mean a lack of sound information about the fish and its habits. Tarpon are thought to be migratory, moving from south to north and from salt to brackish or fresh water as part of their spawning cycle. They also travel from deep to shallow water to feed. However, a true species pattern is not clearly known.

To the fish's broadest advantage, this also means there is no wholly justifiable cause for anyone to kill one. Those slight reasons used to center entirely around man's own vanity. Fishermen may cart them to the dock, but the only one truly bringing them

home is the Southernmost Scavenger Service. The flimsy excuses, then, for killing tarpon rest in that zone somewhere between the charterman's ad only a tourist will buy, and the Kodak dealer.

It's possible to intrude upon the larger spirit of fishing in any number of ways besides pointlessly killing the animal. Not the least of these is to destroy privacy. For example, hardly anything can ruin the tranquility of a day's fishing like a good tournament. The reason keeps turning out to be greed in one form or another, with slices of unresolved ego gratification thrown in for good measure.

It's becoming practically un-American to disapprove of fishing tournaments these days. But if you take an affable, essentially non-competitive, harmless activity, the principal attribute of which lies in the quality of the time spent pursuing it rather than in the grossness of the last results, and you begin giving large cash prizes for the grossest last results, suddenly it's all gone.

Some negate the magic of angling by approaching it from a standpoint of overt, even bizarre practicality: equipment specifications, a humorless concern over questions that have only numbers as answers.

ABOVE *It takes great teamwork between guide and angler to fight a big fish. Especially when he decides to circle the boat.*

RIGHT *This is a giant tarpon weighing more than 150 pounds. A hundred years ago it was considered impossible to catch one this big.*

FAR RIGHT *Like the bonefish, tarpon are incredibly iridescent. Their scales shine like polished silver.*

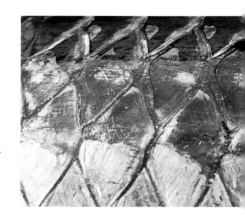

What hook size to use? What percentage of the point should be triangulated? What pound test should the shock tippet be? How long? What pound test should the weakest leader section be? What pound class world record do you want to qualify for? How long should the whole leader be? The butt section? What size line? What's its diameter in thousandths of an inch? How long are its tapers? The belly? How thin is the running line? How much of it is there? How long is the rod? How heavy? How many yards of backing on the reel? What pound test? How tight do you set the reel drag? How long is the boat? How much does it weigh? Its beam? How much water does it draw? How fast does it go? What horsepower is the engine? What's the capacity of the gas tank? How long is the push pole? How many knots can you tie? How far can you cast? How high is the tide? What time do you start fishing? What year is it? How many points do you get for a keeper in the Islamorada Invitational Fly Championship? How much do Minimum Qualifiers count per pound? How much do releases count? If you caught a 73-pounder, a 104½-pounder, three releases and a 90¼-pounder with cheese, what would you have? A large hamburger?

Everyone addresses a certain number of technical questions, but it seems this can be done cursorily, and as a matter of light concern. Attention to facts and figures as if they were really important often obscures the things of real importance, things that cannot be counted, recorded or even clearly explained. In the final analysis, those things will appear as states of mind, wordless, indescribable and of a dimension altogether intangible.

If you are going to replace the essential quietude of fishing with semi-industrial or businesslike considerations, it might be more sensible, simpler and certainly cheaper never to leave the office.

It is now early afternoon and you are being poled downlight over a brilliant, white sand bottom. Much of the earlier haze has cleared and visibility is extraordinary. Actually, you're just offshore from a low, tropical-looking key which shimmers in the heat, its long beaches curving nearly out of view.

Swells from the Atlantic roll the skiff so that it is important to remain keenly balanced. You are in about eight feet of water, somewhat on the deep side for fly-casting to cruising fish, particularly if they are near the bottom. As you shift your weight with the motion of the boat, the Cuban mix sandwich and the three Gatorades you so hastily challenged for lunch press heavily against your tee shirt.

You are in the middle of a long corridor of stark, bright bottom. On your right is the island; to your left, perhaps a hundred yards away, the sand abruptly ending against low coral; there is a thin, irregular line of green, breakers and then blue water. Once, you see an enormous hammerhead cruising the edge.

Visibility is so perfect there is no need to be on the alert for the surprise appearance of tarpon anywhere within a 200-foot radius of the skiff. If it came within fly-casting distance, a three-pound barracuda would look like a Greyhound Scenicruiser.

It is troublesome poling in the deep water, not only because of the depth itself, but because the bottom is quite hard, so the pole makes a clunking sound when it's put down. The foot of the pole doesn't grab well either, slipping off ineffectually behind the boat.

You and your companion see the dark spots at the same time. There is a moment of hesitation, then it suddenly becomes clear they are tarpon even though they are still very far off. You will have a full three minutes to try and get the upper hand on your mounting nervousness.

ABOVE *Poling a flats boat for six to eight hours is hard – it takes skill, which develops with practice and time. The elevated platform increases the guide's field of view so it easier to see incoming fish.*

Were we wrong? No, they're tarpon all right. Eight, maybe ten of them. All big – seventy, eighty pounds and better. Still very far away. Funny how the school changes shape. They string out, bunch up. Fish must be very foreshortened at this distance. So clear. Almost like watching birds flying. Watch footing. Is the fly line tangled? School's turning. Traveling closer to the key. Boat's turning. Good. Must make the intercept. Must take them head on. Too deep for a side shot. They'd see the boat. It's going to work. Looking at them from in front.

BELOW *A Red and White Tarpon Fly.*

"I'm down. Anytime." You look back and your friend has the push pole flat across his knees. "Go." He insists, never taking his eyes from the tarpon.

How far now? 150 feet. False-casting. Hold up all the line you can. Fish coming on, almost single-file. Watch. You want thirty feet on them. No slips. Loops open. Controlled. Cast. Wait. Fly settling. Two, three feet. Tarpon at six. Or eight. Closing. Is the lead fish close enough? Start bringing it back. He sees it. Accelerating. Elevating. Growing silver. Face disjointing. Dark. Has it. Turning back down. Tension. Hit hard. Again. Again. Again.

ABOVE *The Marquesas Islands off Key West are incredibly beautiful, and a great place to find permit as well as tarpon.*

He is already going another way and the strain disorients you so much the
fly line is suddenly gone from your left hand. Whirling, it jams its way through
the guides. You hear the sound of the power tilt as the engine goes down,
starts. Slowly, you begin to follow.

FLORIDA – FACTFILE

BACKGROUND

If the Florida Keys have a fault, it seems to be that they have been over-loved. As far back as the early nineteenth century, people from the northern states were building homes in the Keys and spending the winter months there. The old sea captains quickly discovered places such as Key West, where they began to settle throughout the Victorian era. In modern times, the flood of immigrants from the Caribbean, coupled with the continued interest of northerners and Canadians, has rendered Florida the fourth most populous US state.

The Florida Keys are second in popularity only to the Rocky Mountains as a North American fishing destination. They are serviced by a single highway that often becomes a bottleneck of traffic. The intricate pattern of channels and banks is unique, covering some 4,000 square miles of shallows where tarpon, among other fish, can be sighted and caught on light tackle. The most popular locations are Islamorada, Marathon, and Key West. The town of Key West also provides access to the Marquesas Keys, an isolated group of islands that lies 28 miles to its west. All types of accommodation exist in the Keys, from basic fish camps, to motels, to first-class hotels.

WHEN TO GO

Located in the most southerly state, the Florida Keys have glorious weather for most of the year. The average annual temperature is usually around 77°F (25°C). If it gets too hot in the summer, you are never far from being able to jump in the water to cool off. Rainfall tends to be heaviest during the summer: Key West averages around 40 inches annually.

The peak tarpon fishing season is April through June, and, although in theory there are registered guides available everywhere, during this time it is often difficult to find one without giving prior notice. Many regular anglers book their favorite guides year after year.

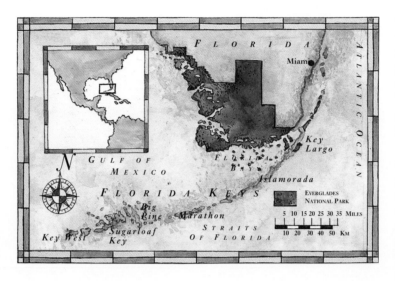

THE FISHING

There are, perhaps, more different species of fish to be caught in the Florida Keys than anywhere else in the world – but this is primarily tarpon territory. Bigger always seems to be better, and if the fish also jumps well, it quickly becomes the best. Fly-fishermen are now trying to break the 200 lb record on a fly rod. The tarpon is undoubtedly one of the most powerful of all gamefish, and exhibits spectacular, head-shaking, gill-rattling leaps when hooked, frequently shattering tackle and a fisherman's ego in the process.

A good many fishermen are serious about concentrating on one kind of fish, while others seem to enjoy catching as many different types as possible. Other than tarpon, the abundant species in the Florida Keys include bonefish, permit, snook, jacks, barracuda, snapper, and even several kinds of shark. Rods of 8 to 12 wt will suffice for many of these – the exception being large sharks. For the most part, it is necessary only to take floating, rather than sinking, lines.

FISHING FOR TARPON: Once cruising or rolling tarpon have been spotted, it is very important quickly and accurately to place the fly in front of the fish. Tarpon are not easily spooked and you can place the fly quite close to them. Allow the fly to sink to the level of the fish and begin to strip it back with a slow, steady retrieve. After he takes, wait until he turns before setting the hook. This way the fly should slide into the corner of the fish's mouth (the softest part), which theoretically sets you up for the best possible hooking angle. Tarpon seem to have virtually concrete-lined mouths, so a super-sharp hook is an absolute necessity.

Point the rod tip at the fish and firmly set the hook with your stripping hand only. Then keep your rod tip close to the water (to eliminate slack) and pump the rod sideways with short, sharp tugs as you pull on the line and the rod simultaneously. This sounds almost simplistic, but if you haven't caught one of these giant primordial beasts before, the sight of one inhaling your fly is likely to give you a dangerously increased heart rate, which tends to scramble all rational thought processes.

TACKLE

RODS AND REELS: Use 9 to 10 ft graphite fly rods which can handle lines from 11 to 13 wt – the 12 wt is the most popular. These should be matched with a heavy-duty saltwater reel and a large disk-type drag system. The smoothness and reliability of the drag are absolutely essential for fighting tarpon. The reel must have the capacity to hold the fly line plus 250 yards of 30 lb test backing. Take extra rods in case of breakages.

LEADERS: For this kind of angling, leaders are designed for durability rather than invisibility, as tarpon are not shy. Tying these leaders is complex and rather involved for the novice. So the easiest thing to do is to buy pre-made big gamefishing leaders. However, if you would prefer to tie your own, a good reference-guide is *Practical Fishing Knots* by Lefty Kreh and Mark Sosin. A brief recipe for a standard tarpon leader is that it is tied in three sections, totaling about 6 to 8 ft. The butt section is made up of 3 to 4 ft of 30 lb test, joined to the fly line with a tail knot. A perfection loop should be tied at the other end. The class tippet is 2 to 3 ft of 8, 12, or 16 lb test. Join the butt section by

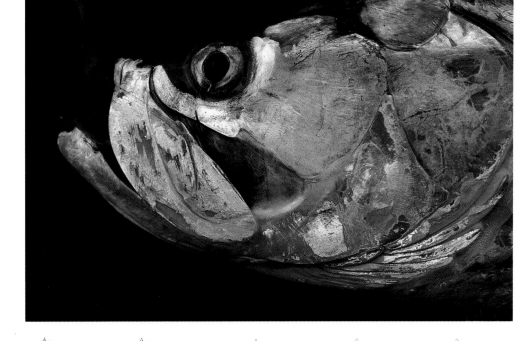

RIGHT *Tarpon are perhaps the ultimate challenge on a fly rod: they take a fly well, they jump high, and they grow huge. The all-time record tarpon on the Florida Keys is 283 lbs, and fish of 300 lbs have been spotted. Even a 10 lb tarpon is a bundle of energy on a fly rod.*

FLIES: TOP *A Red Grizzly Tarpon Fly.*
MIDDLE *A Red and White Tarpon Fly.*
BOTTOM RIGHT *A Cockroach.*

interlocking perfection loops. A Bimini Twist with a double surgeon's loop should be tied at the double end. The shock tippet should be 12 inches of 80 lb test connected to the class tippet with an Albright Special Knot. The fly is connected to the other end of the shock with a Homer Rhodes Loop Knot. This sounds complicated but with practice becomes second nature.

FLIES: When it comes to fly preference, tarpon can go from greedy to fickle in a matter of hours. Slight variations in the shape and color of a fly can make a huge difference in the number of takes an angler will achieve. A selection of the following flies should cover most conditions: the Cockroach, Chico's Shallow Water Tarpon, Stu Apte, Lefty's Deceiver, Whistlers, Seducers, and Tarpon Bunnies. All these come in a variety of colors.

ESSENTIAL TRAVEL EQUIPMENT

Temperatures can range from the low 70's up to mid-90's during prime tarpon time, when there is also high humidity. However, once you're out on the water there is often a breeze, so that the heat becomes more tolerable. It is most important, how-ever, to be especially aware of the intensity of the Florida sun – many a visiting angler has had a fish-ing experience ruined by getting sunburned on the first day out. A heavy-duty sunscreen or sunblock is absolutely critical, as are sunglasses, which should be polarized, so that you can see the fish (and have UV protection).

Remember that the intensity of the sun is ampli-fied by its reflection off the water, and wearing a hat that simply protects the top of your head is not enough – it should have flaps for your ears and the back of your neck.

Dress is casual and you should wear what you feel comfortable in. If you feel able to brave the sun, wearing plenty of sunblock, shorts are the order of the day. Long-sleeved shirts for sun protection that are light in fabric and color are best. A good-quality, rubber-soled, non-slip boat shoe is advisable, with good arch support for those long hours spent stand-ing on the casting platform. Take lightweight raingear for the occasional shower.

The Chalkstream Idyll

England

NEIL PATTERSON

"That mysterious hole under the willow, that dark pool where the weed tresses wave like flags, under that old farm bridge. The chances of a big trout living there are so high, you'd never find my passing these places by in a hurry. As I think back to the big fish I've taken in the past, not one of them came from a place I wouldn't have expected to find them. The places you instinctively feel should hold big fish are the places you should head for with your shooting-stick. This is the best and most honest advice anybody can give."

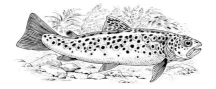

ABOVE TOP *Nick Zoll selects just the right pattern for a finicky Itchen River brown. Streamside benches help anglers with these moments of concentration.*

Above all else, perhaps even more than in pursuit of their contents, fly-fishermen visit English chalkstreams in search of solitude.

In contrast to the crashing, boulder-strewn gorges, the raging rapids and chit-chattering riffles of the rain-fed streams, the shady shallows, whispering glides and secretive depths of England's southern chalkstreams soothe the soul and calm the mind of the visiting angler, lowering his pulse rate considerably.

Surprising, then, that fly-fishers on chalkstreams walk too fast when they're astream. Indeed, I'd go further and say that it's not just the speed at which they travel that limits chances of catching trout (and occasionally their breath), it's the fact that they move at all.

On that sticky day in July, I arrived at the river to find that there were no cars at Sticklepath Bridge. I had the river to myself, again. The sun was hot and I began to wish I'd come down earlier. There might have been a small hatch of something at this time of year. But right now, there wasn't a fly to be seen, or heard. The air was silent. I was able to detect the tiniest wing beat. The thick, morning water rubbed round the brick bridge supports like lava.

I decided to patrol the Square Dance, a compact area of mixed waters, incorporating a stretch of the main river on one side – and Cake Wood. Carpeted with comfrey and ferns and wallpapered by ancient woodland, this shady stream is tucked away behind the Mad House – our small, bark-covered fishing lodge. Here, the sun never breaks through the trees until late morning.

One of the best anglers I met in my first year on the river always used to disappear into an area of stream with about enough carriers to confuse an Indian scout. He wasn't just a good fisherman, he consistently dragged the biggest fish back to the hut. When I saw him set off, my heart went out to the trout. Yet to see him in action, you'd think nothing worked from the knees down. A solicitor from Kent, he was the textbook chalkstream fisherman. Tweed jacket, cap, tackled-out by Hardy top to toe. He was as straight as straight could be. Straight out of E.A. Barton's *Album of a Chalk-Stream*. No one, nothing, could be straighter. I called him Curly.

With his Volvo parked at the hut (doors and boot locked), Curly would go straight to one of three spots – often the same one every trip. There Curly would stay. I had enough time to walk round every likely fish-holding position on the river before he even lifted his rod. But at the end of the day, he'd have taken a heavier bag. In those days, this trout enemy number one paid a princely sum each season for his fishing. I calculated he could have bought the amount of bank he actually fished for the price of a bottle of fly-flotant.

Why did Curly catch bigger trout than somebody who spends the day stream-walking? And why is it so unusual to come across anglers like the trout-slayer I've just mentioned, who fish from a fixed position?

This isn't such an odd question to ask if you think about other forms of angling – coarse, sea, salmon, wet-fly, stillwater trouting. This obsession with fishing on the move is unique to chalkstreams. Why?

Maybe chalkstream anglers are loathe to remain standing in one spot on a river because they have no need to exercise territorial instincts on their beat. With restricted access, their solitude is never threatened.

The beat is theirs. No coachload of anglers is likely to spew out a hoard of green umbrella-toting fishermen, hell-bent on making claims to the best swims on the beat. The fact that I had the river to myself again happily confirmed my theory. Exclusivity, the fact that on most chalkstream beats there are relatively few anglers per yard of bank, is the reason. This, linked with the general belief that fish are always better on the other side of the fence, somewhere else, so keep moving.

But like most of the good and bad habits connected with chalkstream fly-fishing, you can usually trace them back to Frederic Halford. As the prophet of the idea that fishing the water blind is about as sporting as shooting chickens in the yard, he introduced a new concept. Namely, that before you could even start to cast a fly to a trout, you first had to find the fish in question – at least see evidence that it was there and feeding, a rise, or some other movement on the surface. In a historical context, Mr Halford substituted the sense of feel, so important to the wet fly-fisherman of the time, with the sense of seeing.

To his downstream, lure-dragging contemporaries, who spent long monotonous hours anchored to lively spots praying that an obliging trout might just hang on to their offerings (it's no wonder they packed up fishing after the Mayfly), Halford's thinking did more than offer an effective alternative to wet flies. It represented an excuse for fishermen to stretch their seized-up leg muscles. And to this day, the ritual of going out and looking for an opportunity, rather than perhaps waiting for it to come to you, is still as much a part of chalkstream tradition as casting a fly upstream.

At Beech Bridge, I stood and looked across to the trees on the other side of the river. The water runs deep and slow under the branches there and I tried to picture trout that might be tucked under the bank. Big trout, their fat bellies squeezed in between the damp, mossy roots.

This is a slow, strange, sipping area. An area of puckered lips, rather than snapping jaws. Lips sucking at microcosms. It has everything a chalkstream angler could ask of a stretch of stream – except for the chalkstream angler's favourite kind of trout – trout that show themselves, trout you can see.

I leant back on my hands and clasped the wooden bar connected to the concrete and flint footbridge by three metal supports. They twanged nervously. I held my position.

In my experience, the advantages of seat-of-the-pants fishing outweigh the advantages of sole-of-the-feet fishing. Stream-walkers disagree. They say, "How do I know I'm not sitting over an empty hole?" I have to admit there was a time when I could understand this line of thinking. Every time I stayed still for five minutes I'd find myself asking the same question. But after I'd managed to fidget my way through the initial few minutes and settle down, it was amazing how fast these doubts dissolved with the arrival of a trout mere yards from my feet, or at the sight of a fin beckoning me from the edge of weed-bed. Fly-fishermen who use this "empty hole" theory to justify their stream-walking can never have travelled up their river on an electro-fishing boat during the closed season, greeting each scoop of the net with "Goodness, I'd never have guessed I'd find a trout there." It's really quite revealing.

But having said this, I agree that some places are better fish-holders than others. And some places hold bigger trout than others.

Where are these places? And how can you find them? I was standing looking over one now.

The metal railing twanged like a slack banjo string as I settled in for the duration. Strangely enough, I've yet to read a fishing writer who has been wholly enlightening about streamcraft. By that I mean you can't teach anybody to find fish off a page. Think over the chapters you've read entitled "Finding Fish". What can you remember? Like me, you probably only have memories of shaky maps of imaginary rivers covered with Xs marking the spot, the whole effect being that they were sketched at full gallop. The fact is, trout move around too much during the year to be pinned down in this way. From surface food-bearing lies in the spring, to

ABOVE *Waiting for a rise on the far bank, deep in the idyllic sanctuary of the Itchen River.*

45

nymph-bearing lies in the summer, to give an example. Even in the course of a day, a trout may be found in a totally different area in the evening to where it was that morning. It's too much like musical chairs to be coded and systemised. The fact is, finding fish is to do with understanding fish. This takes experience and more often than not, gut feel.

Personally, I go looking for likely fish-holding places with the same enthusiasm as when I was knee-high to a pair of waders. I still rely on the same schoolboy curiosity and ingenuity. I can confidently say that I'm no better a trout scout now than when I was twelve.

That mysterious hole under the willow, that dark pool where the weed tresses wave like flags, under that old farm bridge. The chances of a big trout living there are so high, you'd never find my passing these places by in a hurry. As I think back to the big fish I've taken in the past, not one of them came from a place I wouldn't have expected to find them. The places you instinctively feel should hold big fish are the places you should head for with your shooting-stick. This is the best and most honest advice anybody can give.

Having said this, you may at first pass a lot of spots that look potentially productive but have never produced trout in the past. I suggest you forget the past. The reason why these places don't produce their fair share of monsters is often to do with a lack of understanding of why big fish get to be so big. They manage this because they stay out of trouble. They don't sit out in the middle of the stream in full view of the casual stream-walker. As a result they are rarely pestered by them. But for the reasons I will now give, these piscatorial Howard Hugheses are in mortal danger from the man who sews leather patches on the seat of his breeches and adjusts his eyesight in the manner I will now describe.

Charles Ritz once said that a fish seen is a fish almost caught. Fly-fishermen tend to glide over the big, wild trout because they take this too literally. They look for whole fish, not parts of them. Nymph-fishermen, in particular, miss trout because they don't hone down their observation to look for trout portions, "extracts of trout". Tails, fins, snouts poking out of weed-beds, silver patches where scales are missing against gravelly, pinky warts. The more exacting fly-fisher looks into the river and asks himself, "When is a trout not a trout?" He looks for imaginary trout and takes away the tail, the fins, the gills, the body, the head – hoping something in the tight area he scans

ABOVE *Hampshire chalkstreams are the epitome of tranquility. This is a scene on the Avon River, not far from the great stone circle at Stonehenge.*

holds one or more elements of a trout. Only then can he conclude that a trout is not a trout – when it was never there in first place.

As I mentioned earlier, trout tend to move about in the course of a typical day. Big trout are perhaps the only exception to this rule. But just because they don't commute from one position to another doesn't mean they don't move at all. From my shooting-stick, I've noticed that big trout tend to move to eat. An inch here, an inch there, drifting slowly back, or pulling to one side to intercept a shrimp passing close by. They also move when disturbed, prompted by the arrival of another fish in the same weed-clump, or at the shadow of a bird flying overhead. These tell-tale signs are often only blink-and-you'll-miss-'em glimpses. The angler not there, not waiting for these opportunities, misses them. But what about the dry-fly man watching the surface?

Again, from a sitting position he, too, is able to increase the amount he sees simply by training himself to stop looking for every spiralling rise-form. He must adjust his vision to register changes of light on the surface, inverted dents, shimmers, nervous water. Having done this, the smallest dimple becomes an eruption, and the most gentle, insignificant flicker of the film becomes an opportunity.

This way of seeing is especially relevant to summer on the chalkstreams, when long ago I came to the conclusion that the commonest and most walked-over daytime rise-form isn't really a rise-form at all. It's a sound: the muffled sipping of trout – like Victorian middle-class ladies drinking hot soup – delicately sucking at small insects and nymphs glued to the sticky film. To the man who has been sitting quietly studying his stretch, such a rise is as visually and audibly arresting as if somebody had slung a half-brick into the water.

The amount the eye is capable of seeing is in direct relation to the speed at which it is travelling. The faster you walk, the less you will see. The slower you walk, the more you will see. The longer you stay in one spot, the better the chances of you seeing (and hearing) everything you're ever likely to see (or hear).

This is the Shooting-Stick Philosophy.

In effect, by standing still, you automatically improve your vision. And it's being able to see more opportunities that I believe is the main advantage of fishing

from a strategically placed stick. The second advantage is something I've already touched on: acquaintance with the environment around you. After twenty minutes, you start to get to know your patch as if you were born and brought up there. Even subconsciously you are aware of surface and underwater currents, the pace of the water – all these things add up to better presentation. The current carrying the food to the trout, for example, may not be the current you imagine it to be. It may be one of many different currents on the surface flowing at a different pace, from a different direction. An artificial fly sailing down the wrong current may sound the alarm bells to the waiting trout. The natural drift of flies on the water is often more important than matching the hatch.

As a resident in the area, you're also an expert on the most prominent food-types on the menu in the trout's local restaurant. This is unavoidable. By rooting

yourself to the spot, you qualify as a bush and a good deal of what is flying around will land on you. This familiarity with the food in your area may seem a small point, but often different flies will be hatching off at different parts of the river.

This detail isn't always appreciated by the stream-walker simply scanning the water looking for trout. His scant interest in the relationship between locality and the trout's lifestyle and food-type is often the reason why the stream-walker's fly, which fooled a fish on one beat, fails to catch a fish on another.

But this telescoping-in on a relatively small area of water scores most on summer evenings when fish up and down the river are selecting different flies in different stages of development.

By remaining in one spot you are, in effect, behaving like a trout in a feeding position. Just like the trout you will be aware of what fly (and at what stage of its

ABOVE TOP Rising and hooking the trout is only the first part of the game – keeping him out of all those weeds is the hard part. The River Test, shown here, is a good candidate for practicing your technique.

development) is passing by in the most abundance and, therefore, the fly that the trout opposite you is most likely to be feeding on. It's this kind of understanding and intimacy with the trout that I believe can only be appreciated over a long period of time – a long period of time rooted to one place.

Finally, this approach has one other advantage on summer evenings. It stops you chasing from one trout to another and finishing the day with a pulse rate of 120 and a trout total of nil. I'm now totally convinced that it's not anglers that trout are allergic to. It's moving anglers. By staking out a spot, you have control over how much your area is disturbed, or left undisturbed. The latter is essential if big, shy trout are to come out of hiding.

On the hard-pounded public waters of the Croton River in New York State, where I once fished, the fly-fishers stand over their plots with the patience of loyal

50

dogs sitting bent over their masters' graves. After ten minutes fishing, you start to understand this logic. With waves of spoon-slingers marauding up and down the bank, it's the only way you can ensure that the fish in your area are not knocked unconscious before they get a chance to see your fly. This kind of ground-hogging may not apply to the etiquette-ridden beats in the south of England, but on some club or regularly-frequented hotel waters, for example, it makes a lot of sense.

Half an hour passed. The heat had soldered my hands to the metal rail. As the sun moved over my head, the deep blue shadows intensified under the bushes and a single ring, a ring with no centre, ebbed out into the middle of the river. This was the half-brick I had been waiting for. Evidence of stirrings from one of the many invisible trout in this dark area. Trout paraded like a row of Doric columns, their metallic blue skulls flush with the underside of the skin of the film, as if holding up the surface of the river.

As if built of marble, these weighty trout, one of them at least three pounds, had proved impossible to move – either upwards, out of their element, to intercept something on the surface (a nose breaking the surface might break the silence), or downwards, and thus breaking rank (perhaps disturbing a neighbour) to snaffle a nymph. To the angler glued to the spot, who by now would have noted and inwardly digested all these details, it was time to draw conclusions – and get to work.

The grey specks in the late morning sunbeams, which gave the scene Seurat's pointillist quality to the angler on the move, had more significant implications to the man on a stick trained to notice, rather than simply see, all around him. They were midges – chironomids, just like the ones so familiar to the stillwater fly-fisher, only smaller.

As, year on year, the water level of the river drops, the flow slows down, the water temperature rises and the river becomes more closely related to the contents of a water butt, midges have become a regular feature. You notice these things when you're sitting on a stick by the river, or when you're sleeping next-door to it. I had given these changes some thought. The midge pupa looks just like its wiggly-worm larva in many ways. But closer inspection reveals wings and legs tucked away at the thorax, like a parachute. You will also see small, fluffy white breathing filaments at the head and tail. Fully equipped with the most up-to-date means of accumulating oxygen, midge pupae make regular trips from their homes before hatching. They do this to build up their oxygen store so they can break out of their skin stockings and power back up to the top again.

ABOVE *A discussion of the most appropriate pattern on the banks of the River Test.*

ABOVE *A High Rider Cul-de-Canard Black Sedge.*

At the surface, midge pupae either attach their respiratory tubes and hang horizontally, their thoraxes piercing the top of the water, or they rove, wriggling just beneath the water level.

Compared to a hatch of mayfly, a fall of spinner or an explosion of sedge, all this hanging-out beneath the surface may seem decidedly uneventful. Not so. These midge manoeuvres may not be able to move mountains, but they can shift Doric columns, if only slightly – just far enough for the trout to suck in these squirming danglers, and to register a thin, single ring on the water surface. To the fly-fisher, who is lounging on a stick or leaning on a bridge rail with nothing better to look at, this single ring is a shock wave. It's certainly sufficient to register an opportunity.

To help me locate trout on hot summer days, I cheat a little. As well as my Polaroid glasses, I hang a small pair of 8 x 20 Zeiss binoculars round my neck, measuring only four inches long. I put these between my eyes and my polaroids to shield the glare. It works. And it allows me to confirm any vague distant movement, helping me put a shape to a fin, or an approximate size to a fish.

A silver-skinned circle uncoiled and slithered its way across the river. I received the signal as I was still leaning back on the bridge. I knew where the trout was lying, but not where he was positioned, at least not precisely. He could be behind the low overhanging branch, or in front of it. If only to calculate the life-expectancy of the minute midge pupa pattern I named the Suspender, this mattered.

Devised in conjunction with the River God, the Suspender has a tiny ball of Ethafoam trapped in a little sack made from nylon stocking material and tied in at the head of the hook. This way I ensure that my midge pupa hangs suspended under the surface film like a ceiling lamp.

At the Beech Bridge, whatever problems lie ahead of you, you don't have any behind you. Just as long as you keep to the centre of the bridge. On the back-cast there's all the room you could ask for. Cake Wood meets the main river here; your back-cast opens out over open water. This is just as well, because to get a line across to the gladiators limbering under the bushes opposite means a lengthy cast, a minimum of fifteen yards. A line of that length picks up the gentlest hush of a breeze.

One of the trout tipped the surface again. I heard his stony skull chip the surface of the water and the peck of his beak sucking in a forbidden wisp of air. I hung a long line behind me. Pulling back down with my left hand, I hauled all the aerialised line forwards. Lifting my rod tip up smartly just before it alighted on the water, the line dropped with two deep curves set in it to cushion drag.

In the dark I could make out a tiny white dot. The Ethafoam periscope had surfaced. The course had been set. It was five seconds from its target.

I didn't see the rise. Instead I saw the Suspender down-periscope and dive. This was all the indication I was given to tell me that the fish – at least one of the fish – was taken. The periscope reappeared, this time in a cloud of spray, immediately plummeting down again like a stone. The metallic-skulled submarine was heading for the depths – and the roots.

I had suspected this would be the fish's first, and most dramatic move. I was ready with my response. As soon as I made connection, I began crab-walking off the bridge and down the bank, letting him feel the weight of my walk. With as tight a line as my eighteen inches of hollow, floating Shockgum allowed, I pulled him decisively into the sunlight and horsed him to my ankles. A wild fish with a bottle-green back splattered with a handful of polka-dots, it was one of the last in a long line of a particular strain of fish in the river, a cross between the original river stock and the Loch Levens that were introduced into the water fifteen to twenty years ago.

In the end, it was no surprise that I caught this trout. In the same way that it was inevitable that, from my static position, the trout caught my eye in the first place.

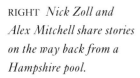

RIGHT *Nick Zoll and Alex Mitchell share stories on the way back from a Hampshire pool.*

ENGLAND – FACTFILE

BACKGROUND

People have been fly-fishing for trout since Roman times, but it was in England, in the fifteenth century, that this pastime developed into a field sport. Since then, the popularity of fly-fishing has helped to preserve the river systems and the natural environments that the rivers create. There is an abundance of fishing all over the UK – rivers across the country are cherished by diligent keepers, who encourage them to develop "personalities" of their own. As a result, there are many rivers of enormous diversity and charm.

Quite what it is about the triangle of chalkstream rivers in the south of England that draws visitors from all across the world is hard to pin down. The fishing is certainly challenging, but it is more than this: maybe it is the sense of the timelessness of these rivers; or the sight of Izaak Walton's house through the trees; or perhaps simply the fact that this is England at its most beautiful.

WHEN TO GO

Owing to the late spawning of trout in southern chalkstreams, the fly-fishing season in those rivers begins on April 1, as opposed to March 1 or March 15 elsewhere in the country. Although it is possible to fish right at the start of the southern season, most fishermen wait until the beginning of May. The onset of the Mayfly Season varies from river to river – the insects on different watercourses have varied reactions to the same climatic changes. Broadly speaking, however, the Mayfly Season begins in the fourth week of May and ends sometime around the middle of June. It is this annual hatch of fly that perhaps typifies English chalkstream fishing more than any other.

This is the only time of year that you can go into a tackle shop and buy but one fly with total confidence – well, almost! The most popular and expensive period to fish, the Mayfly Season is also the easiest time to catch fish and the time when the big fish come off the bottom of the rivers to bother themselves with taking surface flies.

Once the Mayfly Season is over, fishing settles down for a quieter month, to allow the fish time to recover from their gluttony. As the summer wears

on, the fishing is concentrated around the morning and evening rises. During the peak of summer, the trout rise may come as late as sundown.

The season for trout comes to an end on October 1, although grayling may be fished right through until the New Year.

THE FISHING

The chalkstream rivers of the south of England are a rich network of waters that originate in the downs of Hampshire and Wiltshire. Most famous among their number are the Test, with its tributary the Bourne; the Hampshire/Wiltshire Avon, with its tributaries the Nadder and the Wylye; the Itchen; and the Kennet.

The chalk beds of the rivers and the quality of the water provide outstanding clarity and an abundance of fly life. The seemingly endless variety of flies for the trout to feed on make fly selection a true art, and only careful observation and a great deal of patience yield results. Stocks of wild brown trout have fallen in recent years and many of the river populations, especially in the lower reaches of the rivers, are

almost entirely stocked with non-indigenous strains of brown and rainbow trout, which have diluted and driven out the native stock. It is therefore particularly the headwaters that appeal, buried in the English countryside in water meadows and woodlands, where little has changed in centuries and the fishing retains its original charm.

Izaak Walton in *The Compleat Angler* (1653) wrote: "You are to note that there are twelve kinds of artificially made flies to angle with on top of the water." Much has changed since then, but essentially the vast array of around 400 fly patterns on sale today are variations and specializations of those original twelve. Dry fly-fishing *only* is the rule on most chalkstreams until the very end of the season, although some of the first nymph patterns were created on chalkstreams by the likes of Skues and Sawyer, and some beats tolerate upstream nymph-fishing throughout the season.

The brown trout of these rivers provided the eggs that formed the original brown trout populations across the world – in Kashmir, throughout Africa, and as far afield as New Zealand and Latin America. True wild browns have a reputation for strength and cunning, and the clear-water conditions require careful stalking and the greatest of subtlety when presenting the fly.

TACKLE

RODS: As ever, the angler is faced with choosing between power and subtlety. Especially on smaller rivers, carriers, and the headwaters of larger rivers, fishing with smaller rods to achieve maximum accuracy and minimum disturbance is critical. This is the perfect opportunity to fish with 7 to 8 ft rods (cane rods especially come into their own on these waters).

On larger water and lower beats, an 8 to 9½ ft rod may be necessary to reach distant fish. It would, of course, be best to take two rods, one of each, to allow some variation.

REELS: A simple fly reel appropriate to the weight and size of the rod is necessary, and preferably one with a variable drag and with release on the spool to allow easy changing of spools with different fly lines.

LINES: Fly lines should be as light as possible at all times. For smaller rods a 3 to 5 wt double-tapered or weight-forward floating line is ideal; for larger rods, a 6 to 9 wt line. Always remember to have a suitable length of backing line – you are sure to need it.

LEADERS: 9 ft tapered leaders are ideal; and, as ever, the lighter the leader, the better. Of course, the fish will shy from even the lightest leader, but a light taper will catch more fish than it will lose (and often heavier fish).

FLIES: The flies you will need are dictated by the season and by the time of day that you are fishing. Matching the hatch (size as well as pattern) is essential.

   If you can, it is best on your arrival to visit local tackle stores and to ask there for advice. Broadly speaking, however, there are four kinds of flies useful on chalkstreams: up-winged flies, sedges, stoneflies, and midges.

   Up-winged flies form the vast majority of fly patterns, and come in four stages – nymphs, duns, spinners, and spents. Sedges provoke strong rises from the trout and are great fun to fish with, and gnat patterns are often the only solution at dusk.

   From the many dry flies available, the most popular are March Browns early in the year with Olives, Iron Blues, and Hawthorn Flies in April and May, with the famous Mayfly used toward the end of May and early June. Pale Wateries and the Greenwell's Glory can also be effective later in spring, as can Tup's Indispensable. Black gnats and sedges come into their own later in the summer.

   Barbless hooks are strongly recommended to allow for easy release of fish. A small pair of pliers will permit you to pinch the barbs flat.

ESSENTIAL TRAVEL EQUIPMENT

Take good wet-weather gear in case the heavens open. A wide-brimmed hat is good for both rain and sun. A good pair of polaroid or anti-glare glasses can make observation a sport in itself. You should take thigh-waders if possible, as they tend to be needed on some beats where banks provide no access. Always check with the keeper that wading is

FLIES, CLOCKWISE FROM TOP LEFT *A Red Tag; a Cinnamon Sedge; a Blue-winged Olive; a Pale Evening Dun; a Pheasant Tail; and a Greenwell's.*

ABOVE *Brown trout is one of the most wary of fish, making him difficult to catch. He often has red spots on top of his captivating golden-yellow body.*

allowed. Fishing licenses are essential and can be purchased from tackle shops and Post Offices. Both single day and seasonal licenses are available. Always remember to seek permission to fish.

   Lightweight waistcoats with storage pockets are popular, but a small fishing bag is perfect. A net will allow you to land your fish without trampling down the banks: a small, light one is best, as it is easier to carry with you.

A Night at the Black Falls

Norway

MIKE FITZGERALD

"The pool is wide and dark, with a deceptively still, unbroken, slick surface, narrowing to the lip at the tail, and then forming loud, crashing rapids which thrash into a stone wall on the left bank of the river downstream; then they roar at a right angle for a farther hundred yards. There is an ominous black cavern where the base of the cliff receives the full force of this enormous water flow. The salmon have a maddening habit of holding right in the tail at the lip, where the danger of the rapid falls lurks just below."

ABOVE *A close-up of a
Swedish loop reel and
Norwegian hair wing flies.*

In the far north of Norway, 300 miles above the Arctic Circle at the 70th Parallel, the Alten River, now more commonly known as the Alta, flows south to north along a 27-mile course from the lakes of a mountain plateau, and finally to the sea. One of the most exclusive fishing fraternities in the world is the one that includes the relatively few people, other than the residents of the Alta Valley itself, who have been able to fish this magnificent river over the past 165 years.

In today's troubled Atlantic salmon world, it can still be said that no river on earth provides the opportunity to catch such large Atlantic salmon (often in surprising numbers) in so beautiful a setting, and with such a magical aura of tradition and history, than does the Alta. Charles Ritz, the famed hotelier and fly-fisher who first fished the Alta in 1954, was reported by Ernest Schwiebert in his book *A River for Christmas* to proclaim, "It's the Valhalla of salmon fishing – and once you have tasted it, nothing in your life is the same!" Those of us who have been fortunate enough to fish the Alta River share the same feelings.

It was a couple of years after founding Frontiers International Travel in 1969 that I caught my first Atlantic salmon on a fly, a modest ten-pounder, in beautiful Iceland. That memorable evening hooked me for life. I had read everything I could get my hands on about Atlantic salmon fishing before that trip, and it was during this study that I first became aware of Norway's Alta River. Every July a friend in New York received an Alta catch report from Sir James Pearman, who was then Governor General of Bermuda and a tenant on Alta from 1969 up through the mid-1980's. Most years those reports were mind-boggling: scores of fish which *averaged* well over twenty pounds – an average that exceeded the largest salmon I had caught in ten years of trying. And then there were those fabled forty-pounders and tales of even larger fish and epic fights. How exciting yet strange it seemed to me that this all happened from eight in the evening until four the next morning, with "lunch" taken by the river at midnight.

By the early 1980's I was developing a mild case of Alta fever, but despaired of ever getting there. After all, this was the domain of the great and the near-great, the wealthy and the powerful, people who returned year after year – the family of the Duke of Roxburghe had fished the Alta virtually every year since 1862. In the old days, what little foreign fishing was let was given to a single tenant and the entire river was fished with only four to six rods. The more I thought about it, the more I felt it was out of my league. Besides, every mention I had heard of the Alta, since the very first, had always described it as the most expensive salmon fishing in the world (outside a couple of exclusive clubs on famous Canadian rivers), and that made me feel all the more inadequate.

However, a fortunate turn in circumstance was at hand. Through a new friendship with a young European salmon fisherman, I discovered that some of the Alta River owners had heard about my beloved Laxá I Adaldal, in Iceland. They were contemplating some improvements at the lodges at Alta and wanted to visit those in Iceland for ideas – as well as to see the big Laxá, which they had been told, owing to its size and its large fish, was the "Alta of Iceland." This friend suggested to me that I put together a Laxá tour for the Alta owners – and I jumped at the chance.

Four of the members of the Board of Alta Laksefiskeri Interessentskap, the owners' association that preserves the river and its traditions, subsequently enjoyed a pleasant day with me at the Laxá. We had a number of laughs at my expense, not least when I was "guiding" my friend on a deep wade, which I had done many times before, with the Norwegian owners observing from a sheltered bank. Concentrating too closely on impressing the people who could cure me of my Alta fever, rather than on where I was putting my feet, I stepped in a hole with water up to my chin, then bobbed a few feet, before I finally regained my footing. We had just moved a fish, but that was forgotten as I emerged cold and embarrassed into a 25-knot Icelandic wind, to face the four laughing Norwegians. Maybe it broke the ice, because I got my invitation, and the following summer I stood for the first time on the hallowed banks of the Alta River.

I'll never forget the feeling – a curious mix of awe, excitement with a hint of anxiety, and gratitude simply to be there. It was June 24, 1987, and I felt the same mixture of emotions as when I first visited Africa and slept in a camp in Mozambique, where Robert Ruark wrote *The Honey Badger*, or when I first saw the Acropolis, or explored Notre Dame Cathedral in Paris, or Westminster Abbey in London. This was someplace special. I felt reverence for the place and for those who had been there before, shaping the colorful history of this wonderful river.

My son Mike and I were sharing a rod together, and we were introduced to our boatmen. Rivercraft, and knowledge of where the salmon lie in the many pools, at various water levels, are passed down for generations from father to son and uncle to nephew, within the Alta boatmen fraternity. Today's generation have served long apprenticeships, and they take vacation time from their regular jobs to act as guides for the visitors, receiving only moderate pay. All are keen fishermen themselves and they love the Alta.

Mike and I were first concerned about whether our new Alta guides would have any confidence in our fishing ability or would disdain our methods. Both of our boatmen seemed taciturn at first – Hans Ulrich spoke passable English but Randulf said virtually nothing. We were uptight.

ABOVE *Evening light bathes the hillside village of Sognad on the Sognefjörd.*

On the second night over coffee around the traditional campfire at the midnight lunch, I asked Randulf if he spoke English. With a bemused look and a glance at his cousin, he said, "Yes, my real job is air-traffic controller at Alta Airport and, as you may know, the international aviation language is English." For a day and a half we had had no idea, but now a bond began to form.

The next five years were a good time to be at Alta. The banning of drift-netting in 1989, having been permitted along the Norwegian coast since 1974, brought promise of more returning salmon. Sure enough, there was a near doubling of the seasonal rod-catch from 1989 through 1991. Meanwhile, the landowners' association banned prawn fishing, shortened the fishing season to help protect spawners, and mandated fly-fishing only, even for the locals, from June 24, the first week in which foreign visitors were allowed to fish, through to the end of the season in late August. For Mike and me, the first salmon we caught at Alta were the largest we had ever taken in our lives. Now we were on a mission for big fish, and Alta was the place to be. Yet we couldn't break thirty pounds, although several others in our party had taken fish over forty.

Those years were a series of both victories and defeats, fish landed and fish lost, one broken rod with a fish on, and two high-performance reel malfunctions in the heat of battle. The enormous water disturbance that fresh-run Alta salmon create when trying to take the fly invariably made your knees weak, and most of the takes, even with an intermediate line, were highly visible and some actually scary. Twice we watched big salmon lunge completely out of the water to crash the fly on the way down. We experienced the thrill of the near-hydraulic pulling strength of these fish fresh from the sea. Once, one bored 150 yards nonstop directly into a powerful current. Other fish would race downstream, with us on our knees in the bottom of the canoe, while the boatmen steered through the rocks and rapids for a half-mile or more, while we simply held on.

In those days our favorite place on the river was the upper-most Sausto stretch. This section was fished by two rods who were housed in a wonderful lodge framed by silver birch in a meadow of wildflowers. There's a marvelous view downstream here: the river is wide, surrounded by towering cliffs high enough to always catch the light of the June midnight sun. Well behind the lodge a narrow water-fall cascades hundreds of feet as if to complete the setting.

Like the Sandia Lodge, Sausto was rebuilt in 1947 after World War II. Both had been burned down, like the small city of Alta, by the occupying German forces. In the large sitting room, with fireplace and dining table, is a stunning picture of the

ABOVE *Nowhere is there a more aesthetic relationship between land and sea than in the fjörds of Norway, where the "blue mountains" glide to the blue waters.*

60

58-pound fish caught by Admiral W.A. Read at Steinfossnakken in July 1962, drawn by Ernest Schwiebert using black fly-tying laquer. It was especially inspiring to us, since Admiral Read's daughter, Jean Knox, is a regular member of our fishing party. Tormod Mosessen, the boatman who was with Admiral Read when he caught that fish, has been Jean's boatman, too.

One night, on another trip to Alta in 1990, I was sharing a rod with my son, and we were assigned the upper Sausto stretch, from Toppen to Harestrommen. We had two fish, both caught on foot – one at the Tormenen Pool and another from Bolvero, which rushes by close to a place where we pause traditionally for midnight lunch. At Bolvero, the uninitiated would think "no way" because the water crashes over enormous rocks, raising whitecapped waves up to three feet high. Sure enough, salmon hold right in the middle of this maelstrom and fire out horizontally in the midst of the waves, often showing their whole body when coming after a fly. If you are lucky enough to hook up, it's then a fifty-yard dash downstream over wet rock before you can regain some semblance of control in a quieter area below. This is an extraordinary place which never fails to stimulate my soul.

Just below where we sat that night is the dramatic and rather intimidating pool called Svartfossnakken, the "Neck of the Black Falls." The pool is wide and dark, with a deceptively still, unbroken, slick surface, narrowing to the lip at the tail, and then forming loud, crashing rapids which thrash into a stone wall on the left bank of the river downstream; then they roar at a right angle for a farther hundred yards. There is an ominous black cavern where the base of the cliff receives the full force of this enormous water flow. The salmon have a maddening habit of holding right

RIGHT *A guide and angler cross the river and head for home after a successful morning with a nice salmon in a very large net.*

in the tail at the lip, where the danger of the rapid falls lurks just below.

This is one of the few places where it takes courage to fish, and perhaps where the angler is thinking, "Salmon, please don't take until I'm out of here." One of the tales from this place was the angler asking the boatman, "Would you dare to fish?"

"Yes," said the boatman, "if you dare to row!"

To reach where we were, you have to portage around the Svartfoss rapids, tethering the canoe well below the falls, and walk up to another boat secured above to fish the upper pools. During the walk you get a very close look at that short, seething stretch, knowing you sure wouldn't want to go through it. Over coffee we looked across the quiet upper reaches of Svartfossnakken, just within earshot of the falls below the neck. That night the boatmen, Hans Ulrich and Randulf, told us the story of Clare de Burgh, who lived in Ireland and came to Alta as a guest of Seward Johnson. She was fishing with Tormod Mosessen and Helge Jakobsen at Svartfossnakken on the night of July 9, 1968. She hooked a large fish at the lip and managed to keep the fish in the pool for almost an hour. But then, with one long, unstoppable run, the fish was over the Svartfoss rapids. The boatman instructed Clare to lie in the bottom of the boat, and over they went, backward, using the motor as a brake. This feat had been attempted only once before with a guest in the boat, because people had been lost there. They survived, and at the end of the rapids, the fish was still tight. Two hours later, and four miles farther downstream, the fish was gaffed right at the Sausto Lodge, and measured 52 inches in length, with a 29-inch girth. With no scales large enough at Sausto, the fish was not weighed until twelve hours later at Sandia – it came in at 53 pounds. This was an incredible story, told right where it happened.

Later in 1990, my son Mike, aged only 25, was diagnosed with Hodgkin's disease. It was a tough time for my whole family. Mike endured aggressive chemotherapy, followed by weeks of radiation treatments, with courage, hope and

indomitable spirit. We talked a lot about Alta through that time, and I like to think that the prospect of returning was a little part of many things which helped him through the process. His treatment was successful and he was pronounced free from cancer in early 1991, his strength was renewed, and a few months later we celebrated the eve of Midsummer's Night once again in Oslo en route to Alta.

We started upriver at Sandia, and had Barila and Steinfossen, two of the best pools. The water level was two feet high, which is ideal for Steinfossen, but Barila fishes best at one foot or less. On the way up, the boatman decided we should try a quick drop, just in case, at the head of Barila. Expecting nothing, I took that drop, wanting to give Mike the Steinfossen fishing, which held much more promise.

At ten minutes after eight, on about the tenth cast of the opening night, I had a sudden, very firm, blind take and was hooked fast to a salmon. Mike was on the

ABOVE A traditional 24-foot wooden Alta River canoe motors its way upstream though the canyon to Sausto camp which is visible in the distance.

bank, but, as we followed the fish downriver, we lost sight of him. Down and down we went. I was on my knees, but I couldn't keep tight as we raced through a stretch of fast water – the canoe was moving faster than the fish and my line went slack. After a minute I was tight again, in quieter water and, though my arms were shaking from the effort, the fish slowly came to reach and was in the boat. It was very big, later weighing in at 43 pounds. Though delighted, I felt guilty, wishing that it had been Mike's fish. When we returned to where he had been stashed on the bank, Mike's first words were, "I'm glad you got him because I was getting ready to forage for food." Sure enough, he was blank that night at the Steinfossen Pool. Then we moved upriver to our favorite – upper Sausto. We were elated to be there even though the prospects were grim. Like Barila, Sausto seldom fishes well in high water conditions. We fished our pools upriver and completed the portage around Svartfossnakken, which was really moving with the high water. That was our last pool to fish before the midnight break. The little Finnish, aluminum boat (called *Lappi* and notoriously unstable) used to fish this pool was infamous and added to the sense of foreboding. I was deposited on a distant bank to watch as my son and the boatmen slowly made their drops toward the lip.

Suddenly Mike shouted, "I moved a fish!" Until this moment, not a fish had been seen, let alone moved, during that early season in Upper Sausto. Both boatmen simultaneously exclaimed, "No!" Hans Ulrich asked Mike if he was sure – Mike said that he was absolutely and emphatically sure. Unable to change the fly in the swift current, Randulf rowed the little boat, with great effort, over to the right bank. They changed the fly and moved upstream a little. Mike lengthened the line to approach the fish, which held just above the lip.

I repositioned myself so I that could see better and, as the next cast straightened below the boat, an area of the smooth surface of the water, about the size of a card table, seemed simply to elevate about a foot. That was followed by a great flash of silver, an awesome boil, and, in one second, immediately after the take, the largest salmon that either Mike or I had ever seen came clear of the water. By this time the fish was three or four yards below the lip of the pool. The salmon jumped twice more in what seemed like one instant. We all had a good sight of it each time.

The current had obviously rolled him when he took, and he was trying to fight back into the pool with those porpoise bounds back upriver. It was to no avail. He was swallowed into the raging whitewater of Svartfoss.

There was no way that the little boat could traverse the falls. Mike's rod was still bowed and bucking as the boatmen moved frantically on to the rocks. Hans Ulrich

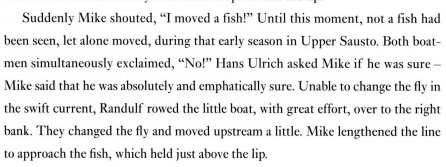

ABOVE *A varied selection of tube flies.*

ABOVE (TOP TO BOTTOM) *A Silver Doctor; a General Practitioner; and a Comally.*

ABOVE *The peaceful solitude of a whole stretch of river and a twilight that lasts several hours. Just you and the fish.*

ABOVE *A midnight picnic on the banks of the Alta, by the great pool, Steinfoss. Many a monster has been hooked here.*

took the rod, while Randulf and Mike ran through the bushes on the bank down toward where the canoe was tethered below the falls.

Hans Ulrich stayed in the water next to the bank, wading to his armpits without waders, and my last vision, before everything moved out of my sight, was our intrepid boatman bobbing up and down, as if on a pogo stick, while he rounded the sharp bend of the falls, holding the rod high.

I couldn't follow from where I was standing, so my only choice was to wait, seeing and hearing nothing. It was 25 minutes until they returned, wet, haggard, somewhat distraught – and fishless. Although I had expected that there would be no fish, I had still held a remnant of hope for my son, but it was not to be. But despite their loss, with bright eyes they feverishly told me what had happened.

Before they had reached the canoe, the rod was back in Mike's hand and he was still tight to the big fish, even though 200 yards of backing had been stripped from the reel. Just as they were beginning to launch the boat so that they could follow, the fish was gone. The leader showed rock abrasion and had parted in the middle.

As we were warming by the fire, recounting the frantic events and marveling at Hans Ulrich's valiant and dangerous effort, he shook his head and said, "You may not realize but that was the fish of a lifetime. He just took in the wrong place. He was well over fifty pounds."

The Alta is a river which may never be the same as in the glorious days long gone when the Roxburghes and the Westminsters would arrive at Kaafjord aboard the

ABOVE *Rushing down countless, lush mountain valleys, flowing through quaint little villages and ancient farmsteads are beautiful salmon rivers on their way to sea.*

HMS Black Eagle or the *Cutty Sark*. In those days before outboard motors, the boatmen faced the arduous task of poling the long canoes upriver – the journey to the upper beats took as long as eight hours. Those on the royal yachts returned to celebrate their great catches with elegant dinners accompanied by a brass band.

Gone are the days of month-long visits to Alta and the incredible catches of yore, such as the night in 1926 that the Duke of Westminster landed 33 salmon, of which four weighed over thirty pounds and two were over forty. Or the 60- to 64-pounders documented on the fly from 1920 to 1949.

However, the Alta continues to add to her lore each year, and still draws visiting anglers who share the sense of awe and excitement that must have been felt by all who preceded them. Five of the seven current IGFA world records (Atlantic salmon tippet class) were set at Alta between 1983 and 1993. Fishing only four days a week for four years in the 1990's, Mort Seaman caught two fish over forty pounds and two

66

over fifty; Alistair Ballantine landed a magnificent 54-pounder in August 1992.

I fished in the summer of 1996 with boatman Agnar Johnson, a storied man, whose exploits on the river are simply amazing. His largest fish on a fly weighed 57 pounds, which he caught at Bollo in 1982. In 1980 he took 33 fish in one night from Nedre Sierra. Most remarkable of all, he's probably the only man alive with two fish of seventy pounds to his credit, one when hand-lining, back in 1951, and another on a spoon the following year.

Even with the damage done to the upper river by the completion of a power dam in 1988 and the interceptory obstacles faced at sea by the Atlantic salmon, the unique multi-sea winter big fish of Alta continue to return. In June the average weight of our catch always pushes 25 pounds – still amazing today. One-hundred-fish weeks, and even 200-fish weeks, still occur for the eight to ten lucky rods who are there during the periods of foreign fishing. Catch-and-release practices, never "traditional" at Alta, are becoming entrenched and landing nets are replacing gaffs. In 1996, the nine fjord trap-nets nearest the mouth of the river were closed, which should allow a return of several hundred additional fish previously lost in saltwater.

Alta remains well-managed under the wise stewardship of the Alta Laksefiskeri Interessentskap, who are carefully preserving the traditions of their forefathers. It is hoped that, with a greater awareness of the necessity of wise conservation practices to maintain this national treasure of Norway, many stories will be added to Alta lore in the years ahead.

In the meantime, those of us who make the pilgrimage each summer feel privileged and eternally grateful for the enduring memories that the Alta Valley, her unique river, and her wonderful people have provided us through the years.

LEFT *Salmon fishing is hard work – it often requires a quick nap.*

NORWAY – FACTFILE

BACKGROUND

Fly-fishing for Atlantic salmon in Norway is very special. Once experienced, it will never be forgotten. Aside from the fact that Norway harbors some of the largest salmon in the world, the magnificence of the scenery is as impressive as the size of the fish. The granite mountains along the coast appear to have been ripped apart and split by the violent power of nature. Fjords, lakes, and rivers are nestled deep in rocky gorges whose glistening cliffs often rise vertically thousands of feet above the deep, blue, rippling waters. Where the faces of the gorge cliffs are more gentle and sloping, and where trees can cling to the rock, the country is densely green with pine, fir, and birch trees. From rocky escarpments above the treeline, waterfalls cascade down from ledge to ledge fed by small glaciers and patches of perpetual snow.

In every valley there is a stream or river, and practically every one holds salmon. The rivers flow through lush countryside where verdant fields are dotted with cattle and sheep. People who have traveled extensively often refer to Norway as the most beautiful and most majestic country on earth, and even a quick visit will tell you why. If you have a moment to spare from your fishing, you can rent a car and drive out to admire the wide, deep fjords and gaze up at the jagged cliffs, stopping here and there in small towns.

WHEN TO GO

The fishing takes place during the short summer months, principally from the beginning of June to the middle of August. Norway generally offers milder weather and calmer winds than its close neighbor Iceland – however, you will be in the far north of the world above the 60th Parallel, so anything is possible. In July, for example, daytime temperatures can range from the 50's to the mid-70's, or even the low 80's, and then cool off at night to 40°F (5°C). A couple of inches of rain per month is the norm. Because of its northerly latitudes, the summer months enjoy 24-hour daylight which can throw you off as a tourist because you're never quite sure when to go to bed. On the positive side, you can fish day and night if you wish.

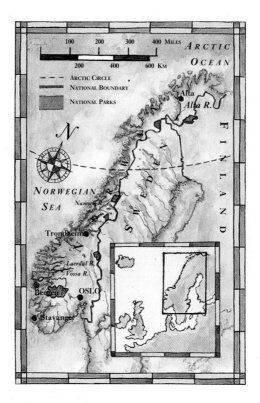

THE FISHING

Norwegian salmon in general, and Alta River salmon in particular, are some of the largest fish in the world. Unlike Atlantic salmon from many other countries, Norway's fish tend to stay at sea longer, and reach much larger than average sizes. This is one of the main reasons that international fishermen have continually returned to Norway for well over a hundred years. The Alta River deservedly holds the reputation today of being the jewel in the Atlantic salmon-fishing crown. Nowhere else in the world provides fishermen with a better chance of catching the fish of a lifetime. In addition, little today has changed since the river was first fished with a fly.

Alta River fish still average around 26 lbs on prime weeks, and on every cast the fisherman has the distinct possibility of hooking a 40 lb fish. With salmon runs around the world declining as a result of harvesting, pollution, and loss of spawning habitat, rivers like the Alta become all the more special. There was a time when the fishing rights were the privilege of royalty in Norway – and even now the visiting angler must pay to access the best water; and, generally speaking, the best beats on the good rivers tend to be very costly. The rivers are usually large and fast, and require good, stiff rods, and tough equipment. Some of the rivers, including the Alta, are so wide in places that they can really only be covered effectively from a boat; but don't confuse this with harling (the trolling of multiple lines and flies).

The first people to fish in Norway as sportsmen were the English, some of whom used to sail their private yachts up across the North Sea from Britain for the summer. Nowadays these waters are fished by anglers from all over the world in search of truly large Atlantic salmon.

TACKLE

RODS: Strong equipment is of paramount importance, and it is advisable to take at least two rods in case of breakage. Your primary rod should be a 14 to 15 ft double-handed rod, for a 10 to 12 wt line. The extra leverage gained with a butt section in the rod adds power when fighting large salmon in turbulent water. Double-handed rods also make casting and mending easier, as well as allowing fishermen to reach difficult spots with longer casts than a single-handed rod can make. Furthermore, double-handed rods are safer for casting the large salmon flies that are popular in Norway. They will keep the fly well above your head, and that of your guide, if you are fishing from boats or canoes, or in windy conditions.

Your second or third rod should be a single-handed rod of 9 or 10 ft, balanced for an 8 or 10 wt line, with a fighting butt.

REELS: Use only the highest-quality reels that are balanced to your rods and that hold the appropriate line. You will need at least 150 yards of 30 lb test braided-Dacron backing with a very dependable, adjustable braking system. Durability, line capacity, and drag system are the most important factors when choosing a reel for this type of fishing.

LINES: You will need different types of fly lines to be properly prepared for different water conditions. Under "normal" conditions an intermediate line is the most popular and useful. However, be sure that you have all lines to accommodate any set of conditions while you are there. Many guides and anglers prefer the shooting-head system, particularly for the two-handed rod. The intermediate, floating, and sinking heads can be changed quickly and easily using the loop-to-loop method, right on the bank or in the boat.

LEADERS: In Norway you will mostly fish large flies to large fish, so you will generally need heavy leaders. In July, you should not need anything longer than 9 ft for an intermediate line, and you may even be able to go as short as 6 ft with sinking lines. Breaking strength should be 14 to 24 lbs, mono tippet for a leader, especially when fishing sinking line. Anglers who are fishing in August should bring some lighter leaders in case the conditions demand occasionally going down to size 8 or 10 flies.

FLIES: Use both standard and tube flies. July anglers should have more tubes and larger flies. Tube flies are becoming the most popular in Norway because they are much easier to cast than larger, heavier double-hooked flies, and they are also thought to give better action in the water.

It is recommended that you bring a selection of double-hooked flies plus plastic tube flies 1 or 2 inches in length. Use size 4 or 6 treble-hooks for your tube flies.

The recommended patterns that follow should have hair wings that are even longer than conventional ties. For the standard double, anglers during July will need flies from size 2 down to size 10. Some conventional, tried-and-tested standard double-hooked patterns are the Akroyd, Thunder and Lightning, General Practitioner, Black Sheep, Blue Sheep, Silver Gray, Red Abbey, Rusty Rat, Yellow Rat, Red Butt, Green Butt, and the Sweep series.

For the tube flies, try the Sunray Shadow (similar to the Collie Dog in Scotland), Garry, Akroyd, or Green Highlander.

In addition, bring any hair-wing patterns from elsewhere in appropriate sizes and colors. All kinds of Spey-type flies, such as the Heron, have worked well in Norway.

ESSENTIAL TRAVEL EQUIPMENT

Take good-quality raingear, including a wide-brimmed, waterproof hat. Waders can be either neoprene or Gore-tex, or British-style wellies if you are fishing from a boat.

Polarized sunglasses with UV protection should be standard, so that you can see beneath the surface of the water and protect your eyes from flying hooks, as well as from the sun.

The layered approach to dressing is wise at northern latitudes: you can either take layers off or put them on to maintain a comfortable body temperature. A waterproof boat bag is useful for holding spare lines, flies, leaders, and so on. Take extra wool socks and perhaps a pair of thermal, fingerless gloves for your hands. Remember to take with you a good camera and lots of film so that you can record your monster catches, as well as the beautiful scenery!

Finally, it is very important not to forget mosquito repellent and a small travel alarm clock so that you can get up on time to go fishing.

ABOVE *Norwegian Atlantic salmon, among the largest in the world, have evolved their great size and strength over the centuries. These fish must navigate huge, brawling rivers that tumble down from mountains to the fjords in rather short distances.*

FLIES: RIGHT-HAND FOUR, CLOCKWISE FROM TOP *An Ally's Shrimp; a Royal Baldrick; a Tadpole Tube; and an Orange Baldrick.*
LEFT-HAND EIGHT, CLOCKWISE FROM TOP *A Munroe Killer; a Half and Half; a Collie Dog; a Magenta Baldrick; a General Practitioner; a Comally; and (shown together) a Silver Doctor partly hidden by a Willie Gunn.*

La Fiebre de las Bocas

Argentina

ERNEST SCHWIEBERT

"It was a deep pool below a heavy chute of rapids, where the Chimehuin gathered its strength, sidestepping an outcropping of rhyolite, and churned into a wild spillway through the boulders. Its currents grew still in these ebony depths, and flowed quietly for fifty yards, welling up again into a smooth glide at the tail. There was a mile of rapids downstream – it looked like trophy-fish water. The light was falling as I caught a brown of eighteen inches – an average fish in such water; pumpkin-colored on its belly, and sprinkled with poppy-red spots."

The storm gathered on the broken escarpments of the Chapelco, and sheets of rain lashed across the truck. There were two riders above the Quilquihue bridge. The gauchos were hunched low on their ponies, their black, flat-brimmed hats and heavy woollen ponchos turned against the wind.

It was still raining, and the wind grew cold as we reached Junín de los Andes. The village stood dark and silent. Its adobe and brick-work houses were shuttered and huddled together in the storm, like the horsemen we had encountered in the road. There were lights at the Hosteria Chimehuin, flickering through the yellow poplars that sheltered it from such *puelche* weather.

Beyond the compound of the inn, the famous Chimehuin river works back across its almost treeless valley, past the cavalry post and the stock pens of the *carneceria*, and the poplar-lined Señoritas, a pool named for the camp followers who live in its bordello and offer company to the soldiers. Its channels split and merge again, changing from season to season, flowing past its smooth wind-sculpted foothills. These hills force the river south into the barren pampas, under a big cinder cone called the Cerro de los Pinos, toward the chalky bluffs where it finally joins the Collon Cura.

The lights were warm and inviting in the hosteria, and its windows were smoky with the chill. The storm lashed through the valley for hours, coming down the big mountain lakes from the Pacific. It had cut power lines from the north, and candles guttered and glowed on the tables. Fishermen were eating beef after a thick vegetable soup, and there were bottles of strong Argentine *tinto*. The candlelight flickered in the faces of the guests, until the room seemed like something transplanted from the stories of Dickens.

José Julian is the proprietor of the simple Hosteria Chimehuin, and his little fishing inn at Junín de los Andes has sheltered an impressive log of famous trout fishermen. Their mecca is the storied Chimehuin itself, which drops fifty miles between its birthplace at Lago Huechulaufquèn to its desert marriage with the Collon Cura, and it remains the most famous trout stream in South America.

The entire Chimehuin remains good, and a twelve-pound fish is possible anywhere in its mileage, although such trophies are probably fish that waxed fat in Huechulaufquèn, or migrated upriver from the desert pampas downstream. But a roster of famous anglers who journey each winter from both Europe and the

ABOVE *The hillside where I am standing is a great location to spot fish and enjoy the magnificent scenery of Lake Huechulaufquèn and the Boca Chimehuin beneath the volcano. The water is crystal-clear.*

United States are drawn to the famous Boca Chimehuin, where the river rises full-blown from the fifty-mile length of its immense Andean lake.

There were three familiar figures in the dining room.

I smiled when I saw their faces from the courtyard. They are there almost every summer, fishing the three-mile reach of river below its outlet. Sometimes they remain for the entire months of February and March. The triumvirate are old friends, among the handful of Argentine fly-fishing pioneers, and know the river in all its quixotic moods.

Prince Charles Radziwill is a Polish exile who lives in Buenos Aires, and has discovered a workable substitute for the shooting and fishing on his royal family estates in the Carpathian foothills – in the duck marshes and partridge fields near Buenos Aires, and in the tumbling rivers of Patagonia. His best trout at Junín de los Andes was a silvery fifteen-pound brown, taken with a big saltwater bucktail from the churning outlet currents of the Boca Chimehuin.

Jorge Donovan is a dairy farmer and stockman near Buenos Aires, and a burly athlete of extraordinary skill. His mastery of Argentine roll casting, which employs a second aerial loop to take advantage of the wind, is obvious on the Boca Chimehuin. He once owned a tackle shop in Buenos Aires called the Boliche de Pesca, the sole fly-fishing outfitter in Argentina during those years, and his fishing logs are filled with trophies between ten and fifteen pounds.

José de Anchorena (nicknamed Bébé) is the principal member of an Argentine clan, whose family seat lies at a magnificent livestock station called Estancia Azucena, in the coastal foothill country near Tandil. His attentions, most of the year, are focused on the sheep, blooded thoroughbreds and fine cattle that fill his township-sized pastures, but after Christmas at Azucena his thoughts turn restlessly to Patagonia and its fishing.

Anchorena held the world record for a fly-caught brown trout for many years, with a twenty-four pounder from the Boca Chimehuin, until it was finally displaced with a bigger fish caught at Correntoso.

These men spend almost every summer fishing the upper Chimehuin. "It's never boring," they explain. "We have seen what the river can produce, and its fish are migratory, dropping back from the lake – and we can see new fish almost every morning, particularly after a storm."

The storm blew itself out during the night, and it was clear in the morning. The sun was welcome and bright at breakfast. We turned west along the river at the cavalry post that guards the mountain passes into Chile. Beyond the treeless foothills, the cone of a solitary volcano rose into a cloudless sky, as symmetrical and perfect as Fujiyama.

"Lanín," Anchorena pointed. "It guards the Boca!"

"It's a bit too bright and clear today," Radziwill nodded. "But when the volcano wears its sombrero of ice clouds in bright weather, the fishing is usually good."

"But it's still good in this weather too?" I asked.

"Sometimes," they smiled.

Boca Chimehuin lies 12,000 feet below the summit of its great volcano. Centuries ago, a primordial earthquake opened a cooling fault in the lava fields, where the glacier that preceded the immense lake foundered on their serrated battlements. Its Pleistocene terminal moraines were shaped against the barriers of these igneous outcroppings. Great dams of ice gathered, collapsed explosively from time to time, and patiently grew again. The shards of ice raised the periglacial lake many times, until each successive ice dam collapsed in turn, releasing another spate of biblical proportions. Such torrents further exploited the seismic fault below the lake, sculpting a narrow box canyon called the Garganta del Diablo.

The Chimehuin still escapes through this narrow corridor in the broken rhyolite, after spilling across the drowned outcroppings at its boca, and begins its thousand-mile journey toward the sea. The winds gather strength to howl down the fifty-mile length of Huechulaufquèn, churning its ultramarine surface into great breakers that roll and crash into the mouth of the river. There is a sunken corridor in the lava outcroppings there, with depths that seem like a water-filled mine shaft, and I have seen a chest-high surf come rolling in. The river widens immediately downstream, where a huge glacial boulder lies in a whirlpool of conflicting currents. There is a deep, riffling reach of water before the currents shelve off into the famous Rincon Grande, gathering swiftly through drowned tablerock ledges, in twenty feet of crystalline water. It is posssible to walk the bluffs above the sweeping bend in the morning, taking a fresh census of trophy fish holding deep between these ledges, and marking down their holding lies. There is another shallow, weedy reach of water downstream, where the river slides toward the old timber trestle, and the throat of the Garganta.

Anchorena circled back along the ridge, and stopped on the narrow sawmill road, just under the monkeypuzzle trees. "Come on!" he grinned. "We'll show you some fish!"

ABOVE *The beautiful Malleo River, a favorite for visiting anglers, flows through the eastern Andes.*

We walked the bluffs above the Rincon, carrying a pair of fine German binoculars. The sun was getting high, and we could see deep into the pool, with every pebble visible on its bottom.

"Look!" Radziwill pointed. "Bébé, look there!"

There are several boulders between the big ledges, and a giant *coihue* log was wedged between the outcroppings. I looked intently where Radziwill was pointing, and finally saw the shadows before I actually saw the ghost-like fish themselves: six huge trout that seemed suspended in air. Anchorena was walking farther downstream. He gestured to us excitedly and pointed to a pocket between the rocks. "He's still there!" he hissed. "He's still there!"

"He's been watching a big brown," Radziwill explained.

"Some of them look like rainbows."

"They are," he nodded.

It was difficult to estimate their size, given the clarity and depth of the pool, and nothing to convey a sense of scale.

"How big?" I asked.

"Most of them are three to four kilos," Anchorena replied quietly, "but the one against the ledge will go five or six."

"And how big is your brown, Bébé?" I asked.

"He'll go seven kilos."

"Fifteen pounds?" I exhaled in disbelief.

"Let's get rigged and fish."

We turned back and crossed the trestle, where the river looped back into the throat of its little ledgerock canyon, and circled past the beach to stop under a sheltering moraine.

We put together our tackle carefully. Anchorena and Radziwill had talked so much about huge fish that I checked everything twice. My rod was a powerful nine-and-a-half-foot Parabolic 19, a saltwater weapon that had come from the collection of the late rodmaker Paul Young. I seated a big Hardy Saint Andrew salmon reel with great care, freshly oiled its spindle shaft and housing, and stripped line into the grass to rewind the pale backing in precise layers.

"You like dacron backing?"

"Yes." I layered the backing line carefully. "There's so much elasticity in nylon that it can deform a light alloy spool, and cause it to seize up."

The leader knot was reseated, tightened into the sinking line slowly, and tested with a series of steady pulls. I reworked each barrel knot too, wetting its intricate loops with saliva before teasing them slowly together. The leader was tapered to ten

ABOVE *Late-afternoon brings on the magic hour, when shadows lengthen and the river awakens.*

pounds. Everything seemed secure, and I knotted a big stonefly nymph to a fresh Maxima tippet. It was my baptism of fire.

I walked up the stony beach to the boca, and waded out into its rolling surf. Big waves surged up past my waist, and flowed past into the big whirlpool downstream. The wind was howling down the big lake, pounding its surf across the outlet ledges, and filling the air with blowing spray. The current came spilling through the deep chute of its drowned cooling fault, eddied into a big whirlpool of conflicting currents, and swirled back past the immense glacial boulder at midstream. Another huge wave rolled and broke, wetting my elbows as it passed, and its wild spume covered my shooting glasses.

"Surf casting," I thought wildly.

There were moments when it seemed like it was raining horizontally under a cloudless sky, as the wind ripped great gouts of spume from the breakers offshore, and I retreated to strip the tightly rolled rain jacket from my vest.

Five minutes later, I was nearly swamped when the surf surged to my armpits, and another great wave broke heavily across my back, sending an icy torrent of water down my neck. Anchorena had advised us to purchase Basque berets at the *almacen* in Junín, headgear favored by solitary sheepherders in the Argentine, as regular hats refuse to stay in place. It took a strong double-haul to compensate for the wind, punching directly across the current to drop our flies quartering downstream. The big flies whistled past our heads – I was grateful for the tempered shooting glasses protecting my eyes. I had been given the best place for my baptism: the churning currents just below the lake. I waded cautiously into position.

"They're a little like salmon," Anchorena explained. "They like to rest just after they leave the lake."

"They lie right in that heavy channel?" I asked.

"Sometimes," he nodded.

"How deep is it?"

"Four meters," he guessed. "Maybe five."

It seemed workable to sink our flies deep into the chute, but its surging currents were so strong that casting upstream was necessary, shooting line directly into the wind. It was difficult to fight the gusts, and a number of casts simply collapsed and came fluttering back.

"I'm not getting deep enough!" I thought.

Radziwill hooked a good fish in the sweeping bend downstream, and I stopped fishing to watch. His reel protested in a shrill soprano, as the big trout bolted and

ABOVE TOP *A Yellow Humpy.*

ABOVE BOTTOM *A Black Marabou Muddler.*

ran downstream. Twice it cartwheeled high into the sun, gleaming like an unsheathed sword, and tumbled back into the river.

"It's a brown!" Radziwill yelled.

"But it's silvery!" I shouted back above the howling wind.

"Yes," Anchorena nodded, "but it's a brown."

The trout was finally beached in the shallows, a sleek deep-bellied fish of about six pounds. It was covered with delicate cross-shaped markings. It looked almost like a salmon fresh from the salt, except for the configuration of its tail, and its dense little crosses of Saint Andrew.

"Doesn't look much like a brown," I persisted.

"No," they agreed, "it's like a sea trout."

"But it's from the lake?"

"Yes, but these lakes are volcanic, with hot springs in their beds, and quite fertile." Radziwill explained. "And they're rich in crustaceans."

"Shrimps or something?"

"Crayfish," they chorused together. "They look a little like dwarf saltwater crabs, but they're crayfish – about the size of a silver dollar."

"What're they called?"

"The Chileans call them *pancoras*," Anchorena nodded, "and the lake turns them silvery."

"I think I'll try them again," I said hopefully.

"*Buena suerte!*"

I worked back into the surf at the outlet, where the rolling surges came tumbling over the ledges into the big chute below the lake. The wind had dropped a little, until I was finally able to drive a long cast low and hard, and the big nymph actually dropped where I wanted it. The stonefly drifted deep into the heavy swells, until I tightened the drifting slack, and worked it through near the bottom. I gathered the line patiently as it bellied past, and suddenly the slow retrieve stopped dead, almost like I was snagged. It was a steady pull, strong and holding stubbornly against the straining rod. It still seemed like a snag, but it throbbed with obvious life, and then the fish moved slowly upstream. It stopped under the heaviest currents in the chute, shaking its head sullenly.

Suddenly it bolted and jumped. "It's huge!" I gasped.

It looked like ten or twelve pounds, lithe and silvery as it leapfrogged downstream. It gathered speed until the line sliced audibly through the current. The reel was a shrill keening that echoed the wind. The big fish jumped again and again, flashing silver in its writhing acrobatics.

ABOVE TOP *A Bead-head Gold Ribbed Hare's Ear.*

ABOVE BOTTOM *An Elwes Special.*

"Another brown?" I yelled.

"Not bloody likely!" Radziwill laughed. "With that trapeze act, it's got to be a big rainbow!"

Finally it surrendered, and I forced it across the heaviest currents. Its silvery sides and gunmetal back were clearly visible in the swift shallows. There were no spots, and no trace of the red-striped flanks and gillcovers typical of its breed. Its shining sides held only a faint wash of amethyst and rose. Filled with a sense of awe, I almost stopped fighting the fish.

"Looks like a fresh steelhead!"

"The lake can make them completely silver too," Radziwill nodded. "It's probably stuffed with *cangrejos*!"

"We call such rainbows *plateados*," Anchorena said.

"Silver ones," I thought.

But I had allowed the strong fish to get a second wind. I attempted to beach it with increased rod pressure, and it showered me with water. My shooting glasses were blinded, but I watched it jump twice more through the streaming beads of moisture. My arms were getting tired, and my heart was pounding. The fish finally turned, and had almost surrendered in the gravelly shallows, when it gasped and the fly came free.

"My God!" I shouted.

I plunged into the river in futile pursuit. The big fish was drifting weakly into deep water, righted itself after a few moments, and was gone. I waded unhappily ashore and my hands were shaking uncontrollably.

"Bébé!" Radziwill laughed. "He's got the disease!"

"Disease?" My fingers were shaking.

"*Fiebre de las bocas*," Anchorena smiled. "We all caught it years ago, and it's incurable."

"Boca fever," Radziwill explained wryly.

The big stonefly was well chewed, and its stout hook was slightly bent open. My fingers were still trembling so badly that I was unable to extract a replacement from my flybox. It took some time to collect another nymph from its Wheatley clip, and I had difficulty manipulating the knot.

"Look at him!" Radziwill grinned. "He's still shaking."

"Might be the worse case we've seen this year," Anchorena teased.

During the week that followed, we took a few good fish, but nothing like that trophy rainbow. I rolled a brown they estimated at fifteen pounds, but had broken the hook

with a low backcast, and it was quickly lost. They urged me to be patient.

"We'll still see the volcano wearing its sombrero of clouds," Anchorena insisted, "and the big fish will finally come!"

Two hours before daylight on the morning of my last day, the fierce *pampero* had gathered again, stirring in the dark mirror of the lake. It sent riffling patterns across the scimitar-shaped reaches of the Lago Paimun, moving in the rain forests of *coihue* and cypresses and bamboo, at the alpine threshold of Chile.

The wind rose and grew, stripping snow plumes from the shoulders of the great volcano. It gathered swiftly, forcing the surface of Huechulaufquèn into life, until great whitecaps came rolling across the lava outcroppings where the river leaves the lake. Wild gusts lashed downstream into the Garganta del Diablo, shrieking through the wooden trestles of the bridge, until the night sky was filled with spray.

Dust billowed high from the cavalry post road. There were silver *pesos* and a brass cartridge casing at the roadside shrine, but its votive candles had blown out in

ABOVE *The meadows of the upper Malleo with Lanín volcano behind, marking the border between Argentina and Chile. This section of the river resembles a western US spring creek, complete with intense hatches every evening. When the bugs really get going, every fish in the river comes alive.*

79

FLY	LINE		LENGTH	NAME	
BWB	ST	SEATROUT♂	7,5	VALENTINE ATKINSON	1ST SEA-RUN BROWN EVE...
2LIVE W.B.	T200	SEATROUT ♀	2 3/4	JIM HOFFMAN	
G. PRACT.	T300	SEATROUT♂	4,5	DOUG SATO	1ST SEA RUN BROWN ll
1ALLHOU 1	T200	SEATROUT♂	6 kg	JIM HOFFMAN	1ST CAST - JUMPER! MALL
" "	T200	SEATROUT♂	7 kg	JIM HOFFMAN	
	T200	SEA TROUT ♀	6 Kg.		
BWB	T200	SEA-TROUT	4,5	VAL ATKINSON	3 hooked - one lan JUMPERS ALL
Royal	T300	SEO-TROUT♂	4 kg	TOMAS STORIE	THE PRESSURE IS OFF
BACK TUBE	T300	" ♀	2.5	DOUG LARSEN	GREAT TO BE BACK
	T200	" ♀	10.3	VAL ATKINSON	ON THE LAST CAST OF TH MEMORIES TO LAST A LI... 23 POUNDS
-TUBE	CORTLAND #9 FLOATING	SEATROUT ♀	2 1/4 kg.	JOHN TRIM	A great even
"	"	" ♀	6 1/2 kg.	"	thanks to
"	"	" ♀	3 1/2 kg.	"	Federico
	"	" ♀	4 1/4 Kg	Randolph	TDF Sea Randolph's firs

ABOVE TOP *The log book at Kau Tapen Lodge in Tierra del Fuego records some very nice catches of big sea-run brown trout.*

ABOVE BOTTOM *The front door of the Kau Tapen Lodge reflects the promise of another great day's fishing. You can almost smell the coffee and bacon.*

the wind. The spent rifle shell was a curiosity, two young recruits from the military compound had lighted the candles, and the coins had been the property of a solitary Mapuche.

The wind dropped at daylight, and we reached the river early. There was still frost in the grass, and Anchorena started a small fire to warm our hands. The sun had still not reached the currents of the deep Rincon Grande below the lake, but it was bright on the monkeypuzzle trees.

"Feels right this morning," Anchorena said quietly.

Carola, Anchorena's wife, had come with us on my last morning, and after we got a big fire started to warm ourselves, she prepared a huge pot of coffee. We sat happily in the grass, sheltered from the cool breeze, talking about fishing tactics and workable remedies for boca fever. We agreed that the only remedy is more fishing.

There was still no sombrero of clouds on the volcano when we walked to the boca, and the sun was getting warmer. It was too bright and the river was still cold. We caught nothing of size all morning, although we scouted the bend from the monkeypuzzle bluffs, and its depths were filled with big trout. We withdrew to the sheltered meadow near the bridge, where there was a lamb *asado* with fresh tomatoes and bread, and some good *tinto*, and there was time for a leisurely nap in the warm grass. I found a sheltered place and fell asleep.

"Get up, Ernesto!" Carola was shaking me awake. "Lanín is wearing his sombrero!"

There was a saucer-shaped cloud of ice crystals over the big volcano. Shadows were lengthening across the river, and it was already twilight under the cliffs of the Garganta del Diablo. We each collected a sandwich, and shared a *mate*, before Anchorena led me downstream toward the canyon. We stopped above the boulder-filled pool where he had caught his record trout in 1966. I asked about the fish.

"It was quite a night," he smiled.

Anchorena pointed across the river, describing how he took the monster brown trout that held the world fly-record for several years. His effortless long casts had covered the pool as he worked downstream, covering the water with concentric fly-swings, dropping a big saltwater bucktail near the opposite bank. Reaching the deep holding water near the bottom of the beat, he climbed out on a boulder to fish farther down. He was working the big bucktail back across the primary currents when there was a sailfish-sized boil behind the fly. The strike was vicious, scattering spray on the wind. It was a heavy fish, and it sank back toward the bottom and sulked. The trout had hooked itself, and the rod was bent in a stubborn circle.

"I knew it was a good fish," he said.

He had no idea how big it really was, but it turned and lunged downstream, wrenching the rod tip into the water. The reel was overspinning wildly, fouling the loosely coiled line. Anchorena struggled among the sunk boulders to follow, trying to unscramble the reel, and fell hard. He had bruised his ribs, tearing his canvas waders, and gouging both knees. But finally the tangle worked free, as the great fish sulked, and he quickly cleared the slack into the reel. The big fish was still there, and Anchorena was grateful for its mistake.

"He just stayed there without moving," he remembered, "and it felt like I was fouled on the bottom."

His spirits sank, and his wounds were starting to ache. Anchorena worked farther down through the boulders, and tried pumping and reeling with almost no effect. He tried alternating strong pressure with slack. The fish still held motionless in the middle of the river, like a sunken snag.

"Just when I was sure he was gone," Anchorena continued, "the fish moved upstream and stopped again."

It was a minor victory, but hope was surging again, and it was the beginning of the end. He patiently pumped the fish from the bottom. The stalemate lasted another fifteen minutes, but as it finally wallowed in the surface, it rolled and attempted to bolt. The reel whimpered in protest, emitting a ratchety little rattle from time to time. There was a worrisome tangle of big deadfalls downstream, trees from the shoulders of the volcano, and carried down the lake in big storms.

It was getting dark quickly.

Anchorena kept pressuring the fish, forcing it off balance and nagging at its ebbing strength. The moon began to rise. Its light helped to illuminate the little canyon, and when the great fish floundered weakly, he saw its immense white belly as it shuddered and rolled. The big trout surrendered grudgingly, giving ground millimeter by millimeter, as Anchorena pressed it hard. It rolled in the rocky shallows, and he gasped when he saw its length, lying weakly at his feet. He reached anxiously with his gaff. The trout seemed to sense its peril, righted itself with great dignity, and tried to reach the current. Anchorena patiently forced it back.

"My arms were shaking," he confessed.

The great tail was fanning weakly in the faint moonlight, and he reached again with the gaff. It was finally the moment of truth. The hand gaff struck and held, but the fish thrashed wildly, showering him with water. It wrenched violently and twisted free, and Anchorena was close to panic. He floundered and almost went down in the river, but his quarry was exhausted too, and it surfaced near his feet.

"I just gaffed it again!" he said.

ABOVE *An alternative excursion across the Andes to Chile reveals some great sea-trout fishing in Torres del Paine National Park. Some think that these are the most spectacular peaks in the world.*

RIGHT *A five-pound brown, taken from a boca ("rivermouth") just at last light, is cause for jubilation.*

His pretty young daughters, Carolina and Paola, had come downstream in the darkness, worried that he had not returned. The girls were on the opposite bank, blurred silhouettes on the lava cornices. But they saw their father wrestle the great fish ashore, and shouted questions about its size.

"It might go twenty pounds!"

Both girls laughed derisively at such exaggeration. "Then it's not really a trout," they scoffed, "It's a crocodile!"

"They thought I was teasing," he said.

He pulled the small Chatillon from his fishing vest, struck a match, and was stunned to find the scale simply bottomed out at twenty pounds. Anchorena hooked the scale in the opposite gill cover, and struggled to raise the fish in the darkness. The Chatillon struck bottom again.

"It's heavier than my scale can weigh!" he yelled.

The girls stopped laughing and went running back along the rimrock, to tell the others and meet their father at the bridge. It was the largest trout anyone had ever caught at the Boca Chimehuin. They gathered around the cookfire, admiring its massive hookbilled kype, and its spotted length of more than a meter. It still weighed twenty-four pounds in Junín.

Radziwill was starting down the same reach of water now, working patiently along the opposite bank, and we stayed to watch him cover the water. The pool had surrendered a world record fish to Anchorena, and it had become something of a shrine. The light was starting to fail as Anchorena led me farther along the Garganta del Diablo.

He stopped to fish the next pool, explaining that its bottom was tricky to wade in the darkness, and directed me to an easier site downstream. There were shrubs armed with thorns like knitting needles, and I skirted them cautiously to protect my chest waders and thighs. I found the steep little trail he had described, and started down in the twilight.

"It looks good," I thought.

It was a deep pool below a heavy chute of rapids, where the Chimehuin gathered its strength, sidestepping an outcropping of rhyolite, and churned into a wild spillway through the boulders. Its currents grew still in these ebony depths, and flowed quietly for fifty yards, welling up again into a smooth glide at the tail. There was a mile of rapids downstream – it looked like trophy-fish water. The light was falling as I caught a brown of eighteen inches – an average fish in such water; pumpkin-colored on its belly, and sprinkled with poppy-red spots. It was obviously a river fish. I nursed it gently, until it bolted with better casting room. It was almost time to climb out from the canyon, before it was too dark to find the steep trail.

"It's just about over," I sighed.

There had been no trophies from the mecca of my dreams, and the week had passed swiftly. I had hooked and lost several large trout – my best was still a four-pound rainbow.

83

"But four pounds isn't exactly bad," I thought.

Suddenly there was an immense swirl at midstream. The fish had engulfed the big streamer with a wild lunge, and the reel noisily surrendered huge staccato lengths of line. The trout bored deep into the heavy current at the throat of the pool. It was a mistake. I tightened to maintain a steady pressure on my tackle, without enough force to panic the fish. It was fighting both the river and the rod, and I wanted to stay there, steadily eroding its strength. The tactics worked surprisingly well, and it surrendered most of its explosive energy in those first critical minutes. It was nearly beaten when it finally drifted back, wallowing in the failing light.

"Careful," I thought wildly. "Careful!"

There was a moment that threatened to turn sour, when the fish floundered weakly on the surface, working toward the rapids downstream. I could not possibly follow at night. It seemed impossible to hold even a spent fish of such weight in the gathering currents downstream, unless I tricked it into helping me. There are times when a hooked fish will move away from the pressure of your tackle, so I stripped six or eight yards of line from the reel, without releasing it from my rod fingers. The fish seemed to stop momentarily. I lowered the rod tip to the current, and shook the loose slack quickly into its flow. It bellied tight past the trout, and hung there throbbing for several seconds. The struggling fish collected itself, and slowly started back upstream against its pull, slowly bulldogging past me in the darkness, and sulking in the depths of the pool.

ABOVE TOP *A Giant Golden Stone.*

ABOVE BOTTOM *An Olive Green Wooly Bugger.*

There was a quiet little backwater in the shallows, and when I probed the bottom with my brogues, it seemed good. The fish rolled again, and surrendered a few grudging yards. I forced it closer, but it seemed to sense me in the darkness, and bolted back toward midstream. I coaxed it back patiently. It tried another half-hearted run, and this time I snubbed it short. It lay shuddering at my feet, until I seated my fingers across its gill covers, and carried it ashore.

My heart was pounding hard.

It was a big rainbow of fourteen pounds, and it proved difficult to climb out from the canyon with the fish, wrestling its thickly muscled bulk up the steep trail in the dark. I finally reached the top, and cut across the brushy little bench to the road. The river lay almost mute beyond the cornices of the little postpile gorge. I stopped to rest when I finally reached the road. The weather on the horizon was cloudless and clear in Chile. The seething constellations were very bright, and I stood there staring at the Southern Cross.

The mountains of the high cordillera were darkly purple in the dying light, and there was still a faint sombrero surrounding Lanín. The vast surface of

ABOVE TOP *A Brown Wooly Bugger.*

ABOVE BOTTOM *A Black Zonker.*

Huechulaufquèn lay absolutely still, a mirror of vermilion and lavender and mauve. Two big herons flew past in the night. The rapids of the Garganta del Diablo were muted in the canyon, and I started toward the bridge. The other members of our party had already returned to the trucks. I could hear their laughter, and see the big cookfire near the trestle. I was suddenly surprised at the depth of my fatigue, and the tail of the great fish was dragging in the dust.

The night wind stirred in the monkeypuzzle trees, riffling restlessly across the still mirror of the lake. There was a tiny Mapuche woman resting with her children beside the shrine, and three candles flickered in the darkness.

BELOW *A sweeping vista across the pampas and the Rio Grande in Tierra del Fuego – the magical home of the world's largest sea-run brown trout.*

ARGENTINA – FACTFILE

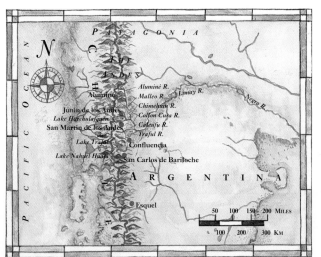

NATIONAL BOUNDARY

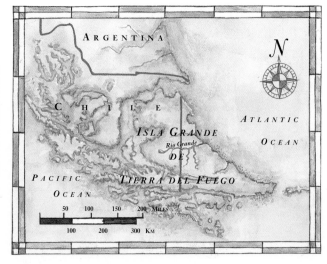

BACKGROUND

Argentina boasts stellar trout fishing, from the breathtakingly beautiful northern streams of Patagonia to the stark countryside surrounding the world's most prolific sea-trout river – the Rio Grande in Tierra del Fuego, the island off the southernmost tip of South America. The success of the fishery on the Rio Grande is a modern-day fisherman's Cinderella story, and the sea-run trout fishing here is now two to three times more productive than it was 40 years ago when Joe Brooks first introduced the sea-run browns to anglers via the printed page. In Patagonia, which extends from the Pacific Ocean to the Atlantic, straddling the Andes, you will find an amazing diversity of fishing. The natural stocks of rainbow, brown, and brook trout rival any in the world. The reverse season delights European and North American anglers alike.

WHEN TO GO

The Patagonian trout season usually opens in mid-November. Depending on snow melt and runoff, fisheries are usually in shape by early December and continue fishing well through the summer months of January, February, and March. April can be cool, but trout fishing remains productive until the close of the season, which usually falls during the second or third week of April.

In Tierra del Fuego, sea-run trout begin to ascend the Rio Grande as early as November, though December to April is considered prime time here, and strong runs of fish continue well into March and early April.

THE FISHING

Most Argentine fisheries are on huge *estancias* or in remote park areas, almost guaranteeing stream privacy. Rivers are extremely varied, and wading is available, as is floating or drifting from comfortable boats, making angling for trophy trout attainable for fishermen of all skill levels.

While trout in Patagonia will respond to the same techniques used on waters elsewhere in the world, you will find that Patagonian fish often prefer to lie in faster water; hence, prospecting with dry flies can be very productive here even when no trout are observed rising. Don't be lulled into a false sense of security by the light fishing pressure on Argentine streams. Big trout got that way because they paid attention to their surroundings, and they are easily spooked. As with all trout fishing, fish and wade slowly and carefully for the best opportunity of the largest trout in any river.

In Tierra del Fuego, the sea-run brown trout seem to retain more of the eccentricities of resident browns than, for example, steelhead do of resident rainbows. Very moody fish, sea-run browns must be shown flies the way they want to see them at the precise time, night or day, that they are ready to take. However, the Rio Grande is not a big river and can be fished with a wide range of techniques, allowing plenty of scope for the fish to be caught. Fishing is generally downstream-and-across, but as fishing days are long, and the wind can be difficult, concentrate on prime periods during which trout are being taken.

THE TACKLE

RODS: In Patagonia, take two rods for general use: firstly, a 9 ft rod for a 3 or 4 wt line; and secondly, an 8 or 9 ft rod for a 6 or 7 wt line. Consider a light line weight rod for flat stretches of meadow streams – fishing this way can be great fun.

The best combination of rod and line on the Rio Grande seems to be a 9 ft rod for an 8 wt line, which will cover the water and give optimum sport from sea-run brown trout. Double-handed rods are increasingly popular and allow anglers to cast a comfortable line with little effort.

REELS: Take a quality single-action fly reel with appropriate line for your rod. Ensure sufficient space for at least at least 100 yards of 20 lb backing. Patagonian trout are large and can make long runs but, on the whole, disk drag reel will not be as necessary as it is when playing big sea-trout in Tierra del Fuego. Your reel should have capacity for fly line plus 150 yards of 20 lb backing.

LINES: In Patagonia go for weight-forward floating lines. These will accommodate even the delicate presentations needed on challenging meadow streams in the San Martin area, and are ideal for long-to-short presentation of larger dries, nymphs, wets, and streamers, on the freestone streams that you will encounter in this region.

Carry at least three lines for Tierra del Fuego to accommodate variance in water levels and wind conditions. Floating lines are typically most useful during early morning and evening, as well as night-time hours, when sea trout are inclined to come to the surface. Take a conventional sinking-tip line and a Teeny 200 or 300. Sinking lines are usually best at midday when the wind and the sun are high and the sea-trout tend to hug the bottom.

LEADERS: For all-round fishing of streamers, nymphs, and wet flies, pack 7½ to 9 ft leaders and appropriate tippet materials in 0X (9 lbs) through 5X (3 lbs). General-use dry fly leaders should be in the 9 ft range, in 2X (6 lbs) to 5X (3 lbs).

For fishing glassy meadow streams with small flies, 9 to 12 ft leaders in 6X (2 lbs) or 7X (1 lb) can save days when trout are particularly finicky. Pack plenty of extra tippet material for all dry fly leaders.

In Tierra del Fuego, sea-trout aren't particularly leader-shy, although people-shyness may account for periods when the fish take best only under low light or no-light conditions. While reasonable stealth should be exercised, your chief concern should be to have leaders that will turn over the array of fly sizes and patterns that you will be using. With floating lines, knotless leaders of 7½ to 10 ft tend to work well.

Leader tippets and extra spools should range from 8 lbs to 15 lbs. Leaders for sinking-tip and full sinking lines should be shortish (3 to 5 ft).

FLIES: Useful wets and streamers in Patagonia include the Wooly Bugger in various colors and sizes. The Marabou Muddler, Muddler Minnow, and Wooly Worm have also proved useful. For nymphs, try the Hare's Ear or Flashback Nymph. For dry flies, try Dave's Hoppers, Humpy, Goofus Bug, Royal Wulff, Tan Elk Hair Caddis, Adams Parachute, and the Blue-winged Olive Thorax, all of which have proved useful season after season.

Sea-run brown trout are mysterious, unpredictable fish, and the only constant in their tastes seems to be a penchant for black. Historically, most Rio Grande fish have been taken on large streamers and nymphs, perhaps because those were most often used. More recently, smaller wets and dries have proven more successful. Therefore, it may be wise to pack a range of flies in various sizes and change tack quickly when one combination is not working. Wooly Buggers and Montana Nymphs are certainly possibles.

Dry flies prove most useful when the wind subsides and during the hour or so before dark. Try

ABOVE LEFT *Argentine trout somehow seem bigger and wilder than elsewhere, perhaps owing to the vastness of the country or the frontier spirit, or the crystal-clear waters; these fish are guaranteed to make your heart leap and your reel sing.*

FLIES, CLOCKWISE FROM TOP LEFT *A Giant Golden Stone; a Yellow Humpy; a Black Marabou Muddler; an Olive Green Wooly Bugger; an Olive Wooly Bugger; and a Gold Bead Harvester.*

Bombers or Buck Bugs in small sizes and see how you get on.

ESSENTIAL TRAVEL EQUIPMENT

Pack and dress in layers. Begin with capilene long johns and a light shirt; next, cotton or light fleece; and then finally a layer against wind. (However, you should take fewer clothes than you think you will need – laundry is done everywhere.)

Waders are a must in Patagonia and Tierra del Fuego. Air and water temperatures can be very cold in Tierra del Fuego, even in mid-summer, so it may be wise to take neoprenes. In Patagonia, several hundred miles north of Tierra del Fuego, you should be able to fish with lighter-weight waders. Make sure that you take a corkscrew with you – the wines are excellent.

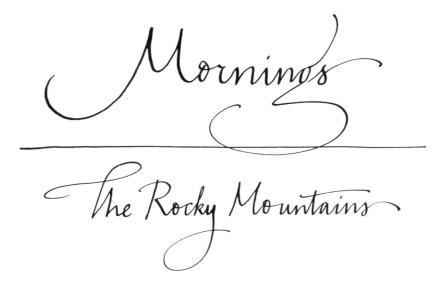

Mornings
The Rocky Mountains

NICK LYONS

"Sometimes the crystalline water was slow and moody or flat; then there were the fifty or so great bends of the West Branch, some tight, some broad as avenues; there were riffles and chops and pools and tails and swampy runs and brisk runs and shallow flats a couple of hundred feet across, all in dozens of configurations, so that there were thousands of different fishing chances. Everywhere, the water was the clearest I'd ever seen, water in which the auburn, spotted forms of the trout and the wavering, hairlike masses of elodea and watercress were ghostlike."

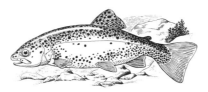

TOP TO BOTTOM
*A Renegade; a Yellow
Humpy; and a Royal
Humpy.*

Every morning around ten, for 31 days, we'd stash our gear in the huge tan Suburban and head for the river. We'd head up the first hill, onto the highest bench, then rattle along the single rutted lane across the fields of wheatgrasses spotted with dark-green weed and sweet clover and pale-yellow prickly pear. There were always clusters of antelope in the fields. Often they would watch us – inert, wary, turning slightly so as always to be facing the car – until we came close enough to be a threat, though we were no threat. Often there were several spindly-legged fawns with them, born several weeks earlier; Herb had seen a doe drop one in the narrow road and he had stopped and watched and then gone around them. "Not enough meat to make a decent sandwich," he once said in his deep voice – the words always curt, final – watching a newborn antelope scamper away, already quick and lithe. Overhead, curlews with long curved beaks canted away, shrieking, and often we saw their chicks, which had no beaks yet, scuttling from us into the grasses.

Every morning, at the bluff that ended the last bench, we would stop the car and get out, and then look down into the valley, stretching off in front of us as far as we could see, with several braids of the river meandering through it like a blue ribbon stretched out casually upon a great green and tan rug. Except for the willows on the inner rim of the bench, near the headwaters of the East Branch, and the ragged line of cottonwoods in the distance, there were no trees: the river lay open and exposed and I knew at once that it would be hard to fish, with no cover, no breaks from the sun, with every movement of rod or line or person taken to be one of the trout's great predators here – pelican, osprey, kingfisher, merganser, heron, gull. An anthropologist who visited compared it to the Serengeti Plain, and it has that same broad fertile space.

We'd have the whole day, from then until dark, to fish the river. We could fish it anywhere we chose – miles and miles of it. We could fish it as hard or in as leisurely a manner as suited our fancy. We could go back to the ranch for lunch, or pack in a sandwich or some elk sticks, or fish straight through, hard, intently. Sometimes Pat, Herb's wife, and Mari would bring down lunch in the other Suburban.

I soon realized that Spring Creek was the most interesting river I had ever fished or could imagine; and I learned that it was loaded with secrets that would take exceptional skill to learn. At first I felt very privileged to be fishing the river, but soon my thoughts turned chiefly to where we'd fish and what the fishing would be like and when it would come and what fishing we'd already had. Within a week, the days blurred and I had to concentrate to separate them, keep them in sequence, though I have had no trouble finding in my brain the full and vivid picture of a

hundred moments, most of the fish I raised for the month I was there. Those were halcyon days and they changed my fly-fishing life forever.

From the top of the last bench the river looked blue, though up close it was green and blue and a dozen variants of amber, umber, coral, and beige; it was really colorless as water in a glass, pure spring water, but it took on the hues of its bottom and of the banks. Sometimes the crystalline water was slow and moody or flat; then there were the fifty or so great bends of the West Branch, some tight, some broad as avenues; there were riffles and chops and pools and tails and swampy runs and brisk runs and shallow flats a couple of hundred feet across, all in dozens of configurations, so that there were thousands of different fishing chances. Everywhere, the water was the clearest I'd ever seen, water in which the auburn, spotted forms of the trout and the wavering, hairlike masses of elodea and watercress were ghost-like. The river held trout large enough to make my eyes pop – mostly browns, all wild, with a scattering of rainbows – which would rise to flies the size of gnats.

ABOVE *The headwaters of Armstrong Spring Creek, Montana, with a first fresh snowfall on the mountain peaks. I once stood in this spot and caught four species of trout – rainbow, brook, brown, and cutthroat – on four consecutive casts.*

91

Nursed on the muddy, milky waters of the Croton watershed near New York City, where I had fished with worms and spinning lures, it all spooked me silly. The river seemed quite beyond the meager talents I thought I could bring to it.

When the wind did not ruffle the surface of the river too harshly – giving it a slate, opaque cover – the water was so translucent that you could see distinctly to the bottom of the deepest pools. What I could see in some of them, five to eight feet down, wavering like living shadows near the bottom, sent shock waves through me.

We would stop at the final bluff to look for the blue herons, which pecked holes in even very large trout and killed many smaller fish. They were astonishing hunters and several times I saw one result of their efforts: a beautiful, wild brown trout with a hole right on the top of its back, as if someone had shoved a pencil down an inch or so, very hard. Herb did not like them. "They can't even pick up some of the larger trout they stick," he said. After I'd seen three with that raw pencil hole in their backs, I felt the same, let the Audubon Society be damned. If there was a heron hunting, it would usually whirl into flight, its gigantic wings flapping heavily, merely at our appearance more than several hundred yards away. I never saw one until it was in flight, and at first mistook the six or seven pairs of sandhill cranes that nested in the valley for herons – though the sandhills traveled in pairs, the herons always alone.

We'd look for several minutes from the bluff, standing quite still and sometimes shivering from the early cold, and begin to think about the day and the weather and the flies and what had happened the day before and which section of Spring Creek we'd fish that day. Then we'd head down the last hill.

Now there was nothing to think about but the fishing. It was a truly remarkable river, but on a given day you could catch nothing; during the weeks I was there, three people – all fine fishermen – got skunked. Once I got none; Herb always got fish. Flies might hatch upriver but not down. The sun might be too bright, the wind too strong, relentless. The large pool on the East Branch might explode with feeding fish or remain perfectly placid, as if it did not contain a trout. The Two Islands Pool might go berserk. The Great Horseshoe Bend – as distinguished from many lesser Horseshoe Bends – might look barren, or might have one, three, or thirty fish rising. But once I had looked into several of the deepest pools I knew something of what the river contained, everywhere, and a shiver of expectation ran through me every time I looked at the water, anywhere, or pitched a fly into it, and still does even now, years later, whenever I think of Spring Creek.

In the deep pools, when the light was just right, you could see fifty or sixty wild browns, of all sizes – a few ten-inchers, a whole slew of fish between fifteen and

LEFT *Summer in Montana is a wonderful time to be alive. The number one mecca for fly-fishermen in the US, Montana has miles of unpopulated streams to fish, and it's easy to let the silence and tranquility work their magic to ease the pressures of city life.*

nineteen inches, and a few old alligators that would go 25 or more. Sometimes, concentrating on some deeply undercut bank, if you were lucky you could catch a glimpse of something dark and larger than anything your imagination could conjure. Was 32 or 34 inches an exaggeration? I don't think so. Several times, fishing carelessly up the West Branch, I'd spook one of those old fellows and it would bolt from a dark bank – black and too slow for a trout, as if it really wasn't afraid of me or anything else in the world, though prudence dictated it move: a fish the size of a muskrat or a dog, coming right past me, black and thick, scaring me half out of my boots.

But Spring Creek was also a place where solitude and quiet camaraderie were possible. It might be a river crammed with wild trout of great average size and great wariness, a place where I had more interesting fishing chances than I could imagine having anywhere else, but it was also a place where I made some great friends and learned more than I can tell.

At the bottom of the hill there was a shallow stretch of the river that the Suburban could ford easily. But usually before we crossed we made a short trip downstream to the right and the Suburban leaned down toward the river and I leaned over Herb's shoulder to see the water. On the way back to the crossing, with the vehicle dipping low on my side now, I had an unobstructed view of the river. The water was thin here – perhaps a foot to eighteen inches deep, over a sandy bottom, spotted with waterweed. Darting across the bottom, their shadows more palpable than their bodies, were a couple dozen trout. They were long and tan – some darker than others – and from the car we never saw them at rest. They were elusive, evanescent; they seemed born paranoids, afraid of every motion, every shadow. I hadn't the faintest idea how to approach them, or how to catch such fish, but they were beautiful to watch in their wildness, and they were very large – some 22 inches or more – and they gave to each morning a kind of benediction. And they always roused my metabolism. I

called this the Paranoid Pool and, from the beginning, I never expected to catch a fish in it, though Herb said there were times, when there was a slight chop on the water perhaps, when the fish could be caught, when you might gain entrance to the Castle. As day after day passed, I grew more and more determined to be skillful enough to catch one of these fish, fish as tough to catch as any I have ever seen. By the third week I had found half a dozen such spots on the river, many of them even more difficult to fish.

Below the Paranoid Pool there was a huge shallow flat, several hundred feet across and twice as long, and then the water narrowed, rushed against the far bank, split off into a back channel and disappeared, and the main current formed an

exquisite run of several hundred yards that emptied into a broad right-angled bend as the back channel joined the main flow below the island. This was a deep pool, braided with a farrago of currents; it held a great head of trout and you could usually take a fish or two here, whatever the circumstances, but it was very hard to fish consistently well and wisely.

After we'd looked at the Farrago Pool we'd head back, then ford the river and rumble slowly up the rutted and pitted dirt track that skirted the dozens of S curves of the West Branch, looking for flies or rises, flushing more curlew and their chicks, as well as little killdeer that hugged the road and then disappeared into the grasses, spotting a white-tailed deer or a cluster of sandhill cranes beyond the fence that kept the cattle from trampling the banks of the river. In places you could see

ABOVE *This is the "ring of the rise": the moment a rainbow trout has just lifted in the water to sip a tiny mayfly. In this case it's a trico.*

ABOVE *Yellowstone Park's midway Geyser Basin sets the backdrop for this angler fishing the Firehole River.*

where an oxbow had silted in, grown grass, and caused the river to adjust its path. The older routes were a delicate, lighter, fresher green than the other grasses. Herb had been advised to tinker with the river, to add structures that would help prevent the silting of bends, but his principle of conservation was abrupt and final: Leave it alone. He believed that the river would change, shift, adjust, suffer, flourish, and take quite good care of itself, thank you. Fencing out the cattle was an exception. And once he and I, on a scorching July afternoon, planted about a hundred willow shoots – none of which survived.

As we drove slowly down the West Branch, we'd hear the ice in the lemonade jug rattle, and we'd keep an eye peeled to the river. We'd always pass the decaying carcass of a calf struck by lightning that spring, and I'd always look to see if it was less of itself. The interior had collapsed and the skin kept getting tighter. At first there was an eager mass of insects everywhere on it, but as the season progressed the carcass kept shrinking, as if by itself, as if it was struggling to get gone from this place. The carcass always made me think of Richard Eberhart's poem "The Groundhog," where that little creature keeps decaying until, near the end, the poet sees merely the beautiful architecture of its bones and then, at the very end, when

ABOVE *An overview of Silver Creek on the Nature Conservatory Section. The stream here braids and twists to form channels big and small. It is one of the prettiest Spring Creeks and is a photographer's paradise.*

ABOVE RIGHT *A brown trout takes to the air as the angler backs away from the bank to keep a tight line. A thunderstorm has just passed.*

there is less than a spot, thinks of Alexander in his tent and Saint Theresa in her wild lament, and about mortality and such large matters. The calf carcass didn't vanish that summer; it was too tough. But it decreased. I tried to find some metaphor in it but decided to let it remain simply a decaying calf's carcass, several yards east of a run that led to one of the best back bends on the West Branch.

In fifteen minutes we'd be at the south end of the property, opposite a huge bend pool that pinched into a slick that you could watch comfortably from the warm car while the world warmed. We rarely saw fish move on our early trip upriver, though we often paused at several of the larger bends for a moment or two. At the south end we had an unobstructed view of a lovely run; its glassy surface and slight gradient let us see instantly the slight bulge on the surface.

Herb usually saw signs of fish first.

He'd point and I'd have to look closely and then I'd see a dorsal slightly breaking the surface, or bending reeds near the far point, or a wake, or the delicate spreading flower of a sipping rise, or a quick black head, up then down.

Herb and I had exchanged hundreds of letters – often several a week – in the years before I first fished Spring Creek with him. Though he did not tie, his observations on fly design, the attitude of flies on the water, knots, new gadgets, leaders, fly-rod length and design and action, technological improvements of various kinds, books old and new, and dozens of other fly-fishing subjects were acute and frank. He fished only with the dry fly and his observations were directed exclusively to matters connected to a fly that floats – but the word "purist" would sound silly if I used it to describe anything about him. He had more fun fishing the dry fly; he conceded the rest of the river to the trout; he enjoyed that visual connection to his quarry – the link that occurs where our world of air meets theirs, on the surface. He could be growly on the subject, claiming that he was a "fly" fisherman, not an "artificial bait" fisherman, but the heart of the matter was less philosophy than hedonism, I think: he enjoyed the one more than the other.

He had clearly read far more than I ever will about fly-fishing and he read with a shrewd and independent mind, guffawing at pretenders and second-handers and people who didn't give credit and "lightweights" (a favorite term of his), even if I had published or edited or introduced such people. An English friend – the author of half a dozen books on fly-fishing – said: "He has a wonderfully grumpy, bollocking exterior which hides a man of great kindness. He is also a remarkable fly-fisherman and makes me feel like a novice." I did not know when I flew out to be with him whether he was the superb fly-fisher the Englishman and others said he was, but his opinions were sharp, often raw, always telling, even when they made me smart. What he did he insisted upon doing deftly. He spoke abruptly, sometimes in half sentences, often with laconic wit, in low baritone. He scared the socks off at least one mutual friend. Thinking back, these many years later, I realize that mingled with the special expectation you feel when you sense you are about to begin the new and unknown was the nagging sense that we were from wildly different worlds, that up close the visit would prove a disaster.

I came full of expectation and some trepidation, and then, as early as that first morning, I forgot what I had expected and whatever it was I might have feared, and thought only of the water before us and the discrete possibilities of the day. The days were crammed with surprises anyway, of the kind that any great river provides, and I could not have imagined what happened any more than I have the imagination to invent a river like Spring Creek. For years it has so dominated my thoughts that I have been able to think and write of practically nothing else. Setting out to write this essay has become as much an exorcism as a report, a private rage for order, for clarity. I want very much to see that period clearly, from

LEFT *Ah, the camaraderie of the picnic table! These anglers are totally absorbed in their conversation about which flies to use.*

99

ABOVE *This license plate offers up a definitive statement on the world of fly-fishing. Do you think there's a 7X?*

LEFT *This old fishing hat now lies at the bottom of the Green River. Only the memories and the photograph remain.*

mornings to evenings, from knowing nothing to knowing something, in all its tension, intensity, challenge, and fun, from when I met the river in late June to when I left it in the bright sun of late July.

In the mornings, when the grasses were still wet with a bright silver sheen and the antelope fled and the curlew flew ahead of us as we rattled along the rutted and pitted track across the benches down to the river, we always felt the nervous tingling of expectation.

At first I wanted to fish all of the river at once, and I felt anxious when we chose one spot. The fishing might be better upriver or down, I thought. It made me uneasy. But after a few days I settled down, took matters one at a time and carefully, and felt content as we reconnoitered downstream, past Paranoid Pool and the big flat and Farrago Pool, then looked at the first few pools on the East Branch, and then drove slowly up the length of the West Branch, noting the carcass and the old oxbows, pausing at four or five bends.

Few flies would hatch until 10.15 am or a bit later, depending upon the temperature, and we'd sit and talk quietly in the big tan Suburban, about books or fishing or the condition of the water, or not talk, and then we'd see some flies on the front window. They might be small dark caddis or the first Pale Morning Duns, delicate and faint yellow. Herb would point and mumble and I'd give a little electric exclamation. Then a fish would show.

Was it a one-riser?

Yes, one rise, then gone.

"Not exactly a feeding frenzy," Herb might say.

But then there was another. And another. It was starting. We'd both make guttural sounds and not voice the obvious. One of us would point.

"Better get your rod down," Herb would say, and I'd say that he should get his down. In a few more moments one of us, usually me, would get out of the car ever so slowly, never taking eyes from the river, unsnap the rod from the carrier on the car roof, select and tie on a fly, and prepare to fish.

In the mornings we always looked and talked first. Then the sun grew warmer and before too long we would find some fish working. The river was merely what a river ought to be – varied, fecund, wild, with large trout, skittery as hummingbirds, that pretty-much liked a fly to look pretty-much like the thing it was eating – and as I looked from the Suburban and then went out to meet it I always felt that the world and I were moments from being born.

RIGHT *Evening on the Henry's Fork of the Snake, one of North America's most challenging blue-ribbon trout streams. Experiencing a heavy hatch on the Railroad Ranch section is something you'll never forget.*

THE ROCKY MOUNTAINS – FACTFILE

BACKGROUND

The Rocky Mountains run the length of the United States, from the border with Mexico in the south to the Yukon in northern Canada – a spectacular "spine" down the whole country, with a beauty that cannot be beaten. Runoff and meltwater from the snow-covered peaks provide household water for one quarter of the American population.

Fly-fishing for trout in the blue-ribbon rivers is a number one experience for fly-fishermen around the world. There's a certain magic in the names of rivers such as the Madison, Firehole, Yellowstone, Gallatin, Big Hole, Big Horn, Green, and Henry's Fork, to name but a few of the famous western waters. These rivers have been a part of angling tradition for a hundred years, and still fishermen make a pilgrimage to these hallowed waters.

The best fly-fishing to be found in the Rocky Mountain region encompasses huge areas of Montana, Wyoming, Idaho, Colorado, and Utah. However, probably the most concentrated area for great fishing is Yellowstone National Park and its immediate environs.

WHEN TO GO

The Rocky Mountains usually have long, harsh winters with lots of snow. Consequently, the fishing season does not really come into its own until the spring thaw has come and gone. Depending on the snow pack at the high elevations (some above 12,000 ft) this is usually, but not always, in June when the water levels go down and the water temperature warms up, encouraging insect life. The season continues until October when the snow often starts to fly again.

Some of the best fishing of the season happens late in the year when the big brown trout start to spawn. The visiting angler planning a trip to this area should come prepared for the possibility of rugged mountain weather. It can and does snow every month of the year here. The nights can reach

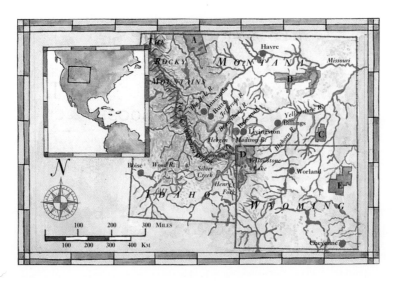

NATIONAL PARKS –
A GLACIER
B CHARLES M. RUSSELL
NATIONAL WILDLIFE
C CUSTER
D YELLOWSTONE
E THUNDER BASIN
NATIONAL GRASSLAND
―― STATE BOUNDARY

as low as freezing, but most of the summertime nights are mid-40's to mid-50's with daytime highs of 80's to 90's. Fishermen can start off a summer morning wearing a flannel shirt, sweater, and fishing jacket, and by noon shed almost everything but a tee-shirt.

THE FISHING

The wide variety of water in the Rocky Mountains presents the visiting angler with many different challenging fishing situations. An angler might find himself exercising small stream tactics in the morning on a tiny spring creek with a 4 wt rod, floating line, a 15 ft leader, 6X (2 lbs) tippet, and small size 18 dry flies for rainbows. That same afternoon he might find himself on a float trip down a major river such as the Yellowstone, and he might be throwing an 8 wt rod with a sinking-tip line, a short stout leader, and a Wooly Bugger for big browns. A serious visiting angler must be prepared for all fishing situations and all types of weather.

Brown, rainbow, brook, and cutthroat trout are the predominant species, with the cutthroat being the Rocky Mountains' only native species. All these fish grow quite well in the clean, pure waters of the Rockies. Fish of 4 and 5 lbs are caught regularly, and the average size is something like 12 to 15 inches, depending on location.

The philosophy of catch and release was conceived in this area when anglers realized that wild trout (as opposed to hatchery trout) were much too valuable a resource simply to be caught and killed. It was discovered that if fish were played gently and quickly on barbless hooks, they could be released back into the stream to continue living. Thus, other anglers would have an opportunity to catch the same fish (albeit, the fish becomes a wiser and more challenging quarry). If the angler wanted to eat fish, he could either catch and keep a hatchery fish, or buy trout in the grocery store.

TACKLE

RODS: Graphite rods of 8 to 9 ft for line weights of 4, 5, 6, and 8 will cover most situations. The 6 wt rod was once considered to be the standard trout rod for the Rocky Mountain area. However, these days rods are being made lighter, faster, and stronger, and both the fisherman and the fish expect smoother and more delicate presentations. Thus the 4 and 5 wt rods now predominate.

REELS: Single-action fly reels that are capable of holding at least 75 yards of 20 lb test backing in addition to the fly line will be sufficient. You can purchase spare spools and fill them with alternative lines for quick interchanging ability on the stream.

LINES: A full complement of different lines is recommended, from floating lines to sinking-tip lines, and slow-sinking to fast-sinking. However, the floating weight-forward line will possibly be the line most often used.

LEADERS: A good starting point for a leader would be 9 to 10 ft leader tapered to 4X (4 lbs), 5X (3 lbs), or 6X (2 lbs) depending on the selectivity of the fish and the type of water encountered. Finicky trout call for delicate leaders of 12 to 16 ft, tapered down to 6X (2 lbs) or 7X (1 lb) – it may even be necessary to use 8X (½ lb). It is a good idea to talk with a local tackle shop, of which there are quite a few located in the general Yellowstone area.

FLIES: One of the exciting challenges in these Rocky Mountain rivers is trying to "match the hatch." Many of the lush, green river meadows produce intense hatches of all sorts of insect life. The trick is figuring out which of several different types the fish are feeding on at a particular time. Take some of your favorite trout flies; but you might want to wait until you get to your destination and follow the advice of your guides before you buy the bulk of your flies.

Some tried-and-tested patterns for western US waters are: for dry flies, Parachute Adams, Royal Wulff, Yellow Humpy, Goddard Caddis, Elk Hair Caddis, Pale Morning Dun, Tricos, Green Drakes, and Stonefly patterns; for nymphs, Hare's Ear, Wooly Bugger, Stonefly, Pheasant Tail, Muskrat, Beadhead, Zugbug, and Prince Nymph; and for streamers, White and Black Marabou, Sculpins, Zonker, Renegade, and Spruceflies. Sizes for dry fly tend to vary between 12 and 20.

ESSENTIAL TRAVEL EQUIPMENT

Dress for Rocky Mountain fishing should be casual and comfortable. Chest waders are standard: either the lightweight nylon "bulletproof" waders or the new breathable Gore-tex waders work well for the summer months. Early and late in the season you might consider neoprenes.

The weather can change very abruptly in the mountain areas, and you should be prepared. It is best to dress in layers. Long johns and wool socks are often worn. On top, a flannel shirt, a warm sweater, a rain jacket, and a down vest are a good combination. Other important accessories not to forget are: polarized sunglasses, dry fly floatant, surgical forceps for releasing trout unharmed, a landing net, sunscreen, insect repellent, a fishing hat, a flashlight, and angler's clippers.

Visiting anglers are must usually purchase a non-resident fishing license. Check with your lodge as soon as you get there, or beforehand if possible.

ABOVE *Rainbow trout, so called because of the red stripe along their sides, are among the favorite North American fish. They love fast, rushing water, and pounce on dry flies like a cat on a mouse. They fight hard and leap often. Rainbow trout are not only found in the Rocky Mountains – indeed, they can be fished throughout North and South America, as well as in many other parts of the world.*

FLIES, CLOCKWISE FROM TOP *A Parachute Black Gnat; a Stonefly Creeper; an Elk Hair Hopper; a Gold-ribbed Hare's Ear; a Royal Wulff; and a Damselfly Nymph.*

The Miramichi River

Canada

Leonard M. Wright, Jr.

"Though the fish comes off at the second jump, I'm encouraged by the possibility that they may be starting to take and I begin covering the water at the top of the pool with renewed concentration. A half-hour later, well after my keenness has slackened again, I see a large boil out where my fly should be and feel a small tap. Too big a swirl to be made by a grilse. I stand stock still and check my wristwatch. He'll be back in his lie by now, but I'll give him three minutes to settle down."

In some ways, fly-fishing for Atlantic salmon (and that's the only way you can fish for them in the Canadian Maratimes) doesn't make any sense at all. For example, the fish don't feed on their upriver migration: their digestive juices dry up when they enter fresh water. So why expect them to mouth your poor counterfeit of something they aren't going to eat in the first place?

Then, too, the expense can be damnable. If you're going to fish private water – and most of the good pools are owned by individuals, lodges or outfitters – you can expect to pay from $1,500 to over $10,000 a week, not counting travel, tips, booze or poker losses. Since a catch of two or three fish a week is about par for the course, averaged over a season, you can figure out, without taking off your waders to count piggies, how much it's going to cost you to catch fish that your local fishmonger might pay you $20 to $30 for.

BELOW *A Silver Rat.*

BELOW *A Ponoi Red.*

And yet, both here and in Europe, salmon fishing is widely considered the stratospheric fishing experience. Men, otherwise sane, travel thousands of miles and spend princely sums, year after year, just to step into a river that, likely as not, will be either high and muddy or too warm and low when they arrive.

However, if you insist on going despite the arithmetic – and I confess I do at least once each season – you can increase your odds by doing what Leo Durocher used to call "playing the percentages." The obvious first move in this game is to find out where the fish are.

Every year, *The Atlantic Salmon Journal* publishes the recorded, rod-caught totals for each river in Canada's Maritime Provinces. But don't rush out and try to buy a copy. I can, as the admen say, save you time and money. Most years, New Brunswick's Miramichi river system produces a larger catch of salmon, all by itself, than all the rest of the rivers in that province plus the totals for Quebec, Nova Scotia, Labrador and Newfoundland combined. Yes, you heard me right, the Miramichi fishery usually accounts for at least half of all the Atlantic salmon caught by anglers in the entire Western hemisphere.

Following "The little shepherd of Coogan's Bluff" formula down to the last decimal point, it is of further self-interest to note that, of this total Miramichi system take, over 75 per cent of it comes out of the main Southwest arm. How'm I doing, Leo?

ABOVE *My own feet and rods as I stand on the bottom of a traditional cedar-strip canoe on a journey upriver.*

ABOVE *The exhausted angler after a hard morning's fishing on the Miramichi River in New Brunswick.*

I have a rather wealthy friend who owns a few, productive pools on this mainstream section. I once asked him why he settled on the Miramichi when he could easily have afforded water on the high-rent rivers to the north such as the Restigouche or the Grand Cascapedia.

BELOW *A Bomber.*

"On this river, the reported catches are 30,000 to 50,000 a year. How big a run is that? On the few European rivers where they have fish-counting chambers at the head of tide, they've found that the up-river rods take only about twenty per cent of a run. If the same holds true here – and there's no reason why it shouldn't – from 150,000 to 200,000 must run up this river during the average year. Do you know what that means? It means that, during the open season of a little more than three months, an average of over 1,000 salmon per day have to be passing through my pools. Where else can I get odds like that?"

The Miramichi has another major asset: it is extremely user-friendly. Since it's medium-sized, as salmon rivers go, boats are rarely called for and, at average river-levels, the wading angler can handily cross it in the riffles at the heads of pools. The river-bottom, in most places, is paved with gravel or small stones which provide safe and comfortable wading.

It is also a relatively shallow river. The average fish holding lie is only three to five feet deep so only small-ish flies are needed, mainly #6s and #8s – flies about an inch long. On the larger, deeper rivers, anglers often have to resort to huge #1/0s or #3/0s to get the salmon's attention. Such lures look like humming-birds impaled on meat-hooks and are brutes to cast.

And casting is the name of the game when you're salmon fishing. There's an old saying that it takes a thousand casts to raise a fish – and even that may refer to the good old days. If you figure three or four casts a minute, that adds up to one stingy rise in a hard, half-day of fishing, and landing, or even hooking, that one riser is far from a sure thing.

The standard presentation is to cast an underwater or wet fly across and downstream at a 45-degree angle and allow it to swing in an arc until it dangles directly below you. Then you take a giant-step downstream and repeat the process until you've covered all the likely fish-holding water in the pool. Of course, if the water is quite slow, you cast at a wider angle to hurry it along and you cut a smaller slice in fast water to slow it down. The trick is that, no matter what the current may be

BELOW *A Silver Stoat.*

ABOVE *On a frosty morning, frustrations are aired, quite literally, on a streamside picnic table.*

RIGHT *A composition of flies, reels, and lines, created as I wait patiently for a fish to bite.*

doing, you should control your fly so that it moves at that special, impossible-to-describe speed of travel salmon seem to prefer.

Having said that this is a handy-sized river to fish, I don't want to imply that it's a Mickey Mouse one. Even in its middle reaches, riffles and runs average over a hundred feet wide and pools run from 150 to over 200 feet.

The main Southwest stretches some hundred miles above its head of tide at Quarryville so it's an extensive waterway. And its major tributaries – the Northwest, the Little Southwest, the Dungarvon, the Renous and the Cains – average about fifty miles long and are respectable fisheries in their own rights.

While the local scenery lacks the more dramatic contours of Nova Scotia to the east, it is, nonetheless, pleasant, rolling country with well-wooded hills and meadows, which were once working farms, carpeting the valley floor. This is productive hunting, as well as fishing, terrain. There are plenty of grouse and woodcocks in the thickets. You see moose occasionally, deer frequently, and black bear almost certainly if you visit a town dump at dusk.

The Miramichi has always been the nearest-to-affordable salmon river in Canada because it is known as a "little fish" river that is decidedly "grilsey." A grilse is a salmon weighing only three to five pounds because it has spent only a single winter packing on weight in the Arctic feeding grounds. A mature salmon, which will usually weigh about ten pounds and occasionally reaches fifty, has spent two or more winters up north gorging on shrimp, capelin, and herring. The

ABOVE TOP *A high-jumping salmon throws off spray at Sutter's Pool on the Miramichi River.*

109

Miramichi delivers at least three grilse for every true salmon and the majority of its adult fish fall into the modest, eight-to-twelve-pound range, so Miramichi fish can't average over five or six pounds.

The bigger, more pricey rivers to the north show a far higher salmon-to-grilse ratio and the salmon themselves average much heavier. The median weight of fish taken on the Moise or the Grand Cascapedia, for example, would be about twenty pounds and fish well over thirty pounds are not uncommon. Moise angler and famed adman, Ted Bates, once killed three salmon, each over 35 pounds, before lunch one day. Traditionally, big-fish rivers can command extortionate prices.

Recent regulations may change all this, however, and riparian owners on the Miramichi may see their fortunes rising. In the Province of New Brunswick, all fish over 25 inches long – meaning all mature, two-winter salmon – must be returned to the river, unharmed. In Quebec, only one fish a day may be landed and that one

RIGHT *Bill Taylor of the Atlantic Salmon Federation playing a large salmon on the Grand Cascapedia River in Quebec. The guide stands by with the net.*

must be kept. Suppose an angler on, say, the Matapedia, lands a small grilse at nine in the morning. He's out of the river for the rest of the day with not much to show for his big-fish fee.

A Miramichi angler, on the other hand, can land four fish in a day – release two and keep two – before he limits out. True, he can't keep any of his larger fish, but he can enjoy the excitement of hooking and playing them which is really what most anglers go up there for in the first place.

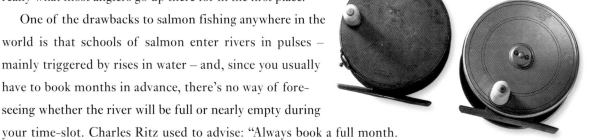

One of the drawbacks to salmon fishing anywhere in the world is that schools of salmon enter rivers in pulses – mainly triggered by rises in water – and, since you usually have to book months in advance, there's no way of fore-seeing whether the river will be full or nearly empty during your time-slot. Charles Ritz used to advise: "Always book a full month.

BELOW A moment of great relief: Bill Taylor's fish is in the net – and what a fish it is!

LEFT *The release of a beautiful hen fish caught on the Bonaventure River. This river has the cleanest water on the Gaspé Bay peninsula.*

That way you can be sure you have at least one good week." Thanks a lot, Charlie – I'll do just that when they abolish the IRS.

While we're back on the subject of money, I should point out that there are ways to fish the Miramichi on the cheap. About a third of the pools are "Crown water" – an obsolete term because they used to be considered the property of the "Bloody Queen" but are now provincial property and open to all licensed anglers resident or non-resident.

If you fish this open water, your costs can be modest. Your non-resident license is $50 per week – $100 for the season – and you must, by law, engage a local guide for $50 a day, plus tip. However, he may guide three fishermen so the cost to an individual is hardly ruinous. Hotel rooms and meals cost about the same as in the States. If you really want to bare-bones it, your guide will probably tell you which families in town will take in angler/boarders.

Be warned that this will not provide a "gracious living" experience. If there's a run of salmon coming through, and you always hope for one, an open-water pool may be lined by ten to fifteen anglers on each side spaced less than fifty feet apart. Each conga-line moves slowly down the pool, the bottom end continually peeling off to start in again at the top. If you move down too slowly, the man behind you will noisily rip his fly out of the water within inches of your precious waders. You'll get the pace, and the message, quickly enough.

If you stay at a lodge with private water, however, you'll have far greater

LEFT (TOP TO BOTTOM) *A Muddler; a Ponoi Green; a Yellow Wiggler; a Cosseboom; and a Blue Doctor.*

freedom of movement. You won't have to race to a pool at daybreak hoping to get in a couple of run-throughs before the stampede begins, either. At most camps, breakfasts are hearty, leisurely meals and the morning fishing usually starts at the civilized hour of 9 am and ends before a 1 pm lunch.

Typically, four rods will be assigned to a pool, two on each side, which allows plenty of elbow-room when fished in the usual, cast-step-down-cast manner. If, say, four of the fish resting up in the pool that morning are in a mood to take, your odds are far better than if you're sharing them with twenty to thirty others. You probably get what you pay for.

Results of a morning's fishing are totally unpredictable because nobody can foretell how many salmon will be lying up in the pool you're going to fish or what sort of mood they'll be in. A lot depends on water levels and weather patterns. My first morning's salmon fishing during early July last year was fairly typical.

The water is clear, but about a foot higher than normal summer level due to a soaking rain two days earlier. A few fish may travel on through without stopping with this much water, but most will take up resting lies in the pool rather than running the shallow bar at the head of the pool in bright sunlight.

The guide suggests that I start, half-way down in the pool, and walks 100 yards up to the head of it to coach the other angler who has never fished for salmon before. He knows I've been at it for years and have fished this particular pool dozens of times, so he leaves me to fend for myself.

Which fly should I tie on? I have three boxes in my vest containing an over-kill of 250 flies even though I know I'll tie on only six to eight old favorites during the entire week. I finger a #8 Conrad – a time-tested, hairwing pattern that's all black except for a green butt – but decide that, with the river up, a slightly larger #6 would be a shrewder choice.

I start angling seventy-foot casts about sixty degrees across stream, watching the end of my line to gauge the speed of my fly. When I get it right, I am full of anticipation, expecting a fish to tighten my line at any moment.

Forty-five minutes later, however, my acute expectation is sagging. As I reel in at the tail end of the beat, I hear a shout upriver, then see a grilse leap two feet out of water. The rookie has hooked a fish in water I'd just covered. So much for years of experience!

Though the fish comes off at the second jump, I'm encouraged by the possibil-ity that they may be starting to take and I begin covering the water at the top of the

BELOW *Richard Adams, probably the most famous fishing guide in Atlantic salmon history, has fished and guided on his beloved Matapedia river for over sixty years. He is truly a legend in his own time.*

pool with renewed concentration. A half-hour later, well after my keenness has slackened again, I see a large boil out where my fly should be and feel a small tap. Too big a swirl to be made by a grilse. I stand stock still and check my wristwatch. He'll be back in his lie by now, but I'll give him three minutes to settle down.

I shoot out a cast of exactly the same length and angle as the previous one and hold my breath as the fly starts its swing. Nothing. I repeat three times without result, then strip in the line and change to a smaller #8 of the same pattern. No action. I change again to a brighter Jock Scott of the same size. Nothing doing. I admit defeat and switch back to my original pattern and start on down the pool.

My concentration wanes again and I cover the water mechanically. When I reach this "nth" degree of boredom, old songs or even nursery rhymes often pop into my head, playing over and over again like a broken record. Today is "The-bear-went-over-the-mountain" day and, try as I will, I can't turn the music off. I am down to the lowest, slowest part of the pool and finishing my hundredth "to see what he could see" when my line slowly begins to rise, my rod-tip starts to bend and then I feel solid weight as my line starts cutting upriver. Salmon have a habit of taking when your mind is elsewhere and you least expect them.

It's another grilse, but a big, fat one that will push five pounds and, three jumps and five minutes later, the guide has him in the net. There's still a half-hour till lunchtime, but there's no more action.

Walking back up the hill to the lodge, I ask myself the eternal salmon-fishing question: why did that fish take? Was it because I had chosen the right pattern and swung it past him at the proper speed? Or was it pure, blind luck? In a rare burst of honesty, I have to concede that it was probably fifty-fifty.

Well, that's salmon fishing for you. Like flying coast to coast, it's hours of utter monotony punctuated by moments when your heart is in your mouth.

Knowing all this, do you still want to try it? All right, but be warned that salmon fishing is like "that first, fatal glass of beer" or that first teenage puff on a ciga-rette. If you catch a fish, you're at risk. Kill several and you're most certainly a goner.

But maybe I'm not too objective on the subject. After all – and shame on me – I've never been able to quit smoking, either.

LEFT *A proud angler hand-tails a salmon on the Grand Cascapedia River. Note the two-handed rod. These rods are gaining in popularity for their ease of line handling and efficiency in covering the water.*

BELOW *Hope springs eternal in the hearts and minds of fishermen.*

CANADA: FACTFILE

BACKGROUND

Canada has some of the finest fishing in the world, with a large diversity of fish species. The country itself is so large, in fact, with so many wonderfully rich fishing resources, that we have covered only a limited area in this book, focusing on the eastern side of Canada and the Atlantic salmon fisheries.

There are some 400 salmon rivers in eastern Canada, providing an immense wealth and diversity of fishing. The regions of New Brunswick and Quebec provide the setting for the visual feast of Canadian rivers in this chapter. They are the Miramichi River, the Restigouche, the Grand Cascapedia, the Matapedia, and the Bonaventure. These are some of the classic, blue-ribbon rivers of the Atlantic salmon domain. It must be noted that Atlantic salmon as a species have, over the years, fallen prey to a whole series of unfortunate circumstances, which have meant that every year the annual salmon runs become smaller and smaller. Contributory factors are over-harvesting by commercial fisheries, clear cutting of forests, erosion, mismanagement, acid rain, and water diversions, all of which damage the fragile environment in which the fish live. However, Canada is one country whose reputation for the conservation of Atlantic salmon stocks enjoys international regard.

If you would like to learn more about the world of Atlantic salmon and about what you can do to help restore this magnificent gamefish, you can join the Atlantic Salmon Federation, which publishes a quarterly journal. This very worthy organization is located in St Andrews, New Brunswick, PO Box 429, Canada EOG 2XO.

WHEN TO GO

The Canadian fishing season begins in June and, depending on the river, usually peaks either the last half of June or the first half of July. However, fishing conditions throughout the summer and fall season can be excellent too. The end of the season can

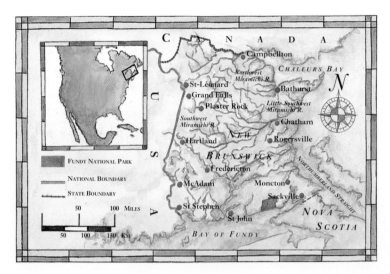

vary from river to river. State regulations may also apply. Nights and mornings are usually cool, sometimes down to the 40's. Daytime temperatures can reach the mid-80's.

THE FISHING

More Atlantic salmon are taken on New Brunswick's rivers than in any other province, and the Miramichi is the highest-yielding salmon river in North America. It is also the most popular with visiting anglers, being regarded as a "friendly river." For years it was known as a grilse river (grilse are one-year sea fish that weigh from 3 to 5 lbs). But since the mid-1970's an increasing number of large salmon have also appeared.

If the Miramichi yields the largest catch figures, then rivers such as the Restigouche, the Grand Cascapedia, and the Matapedia can yield the largest fish. These rivers produce salmon in the 20 to 30 lb class, or larger. The Bonaventure River has the clearest water of them all.

Because regulations and restrictions vary greatly between provinces and rivers, the angler anticipating a visit to Canada should check with an experienced agency or the local authorities beforehand. For example, some rivers require anglers to have guides, others do not; some waters are private, some public; on some rivers you can keep salmon, on others you can keep only grilse.

On most of the larger rivers, the fishing is

exercised from 26 ft canoes, which are called Gaspé riverboats. The guides simply hold the boats within easy casting distance of known lies and the angler stands mid-canoe and casts for a while. If nothing happens the guides will make what is called a drop – letting the boat drift down slightly to the next bit of holding water. The exception to this is the Miramichi, where the canoes may be used only to travel from pool to pool. All fishing on the Miramichi must be by wading.

Whether fishing with the wet fly or dry fly, methodically working the water is the key to catching salmon. Beginning with short casts, the angler lets his or her fly drift over known or unseen lies, letting it swing downstream before retrieving and repeating the cast. If a fish does not show, the next series of casts should be lengthened a few feet, and then extended on subsequent casts until all likely spots are covered. If a salmon flashes or moves near the fly, that particular cast should be repeated at exactly the same angle and distance. When one area has been covered, the angler wades to the next pool and repeats the same casting pattern. While wading in shallow water, you can approach salmon much more closely than trout, so be alert even when making short casts.

THE TACKLE

RODS: Both single- and double-handed rods are used in Canada. They range in length from 9 to 10 ft for a single-handed rod for 8 to 10 wt lines, to between 12 and 15 ft for double-handed rods for 10 to 12 wt lines. On the bigger rivers the double-handed rods will cover more water more effectively, with less effort.

REELS: Heavy-duty reels with sturdy, adjustable drag systems and a capacity of at least 150 to 200 yards of backing, plus the appropriate fly line, are needed for these powerful fish. A fish of 25 lbs or more in a fast pool can run a long way before you can catch up.

LEADERS: Atlantic salmon are not leader-shy, so 7 to 9 ft of leader is usually adequate, with a tippet strength of between 10 lb and 20 lb test, depending on the river you are fishing and the current conditions.

FLIES: The modernization of the salmon fly in North America was basically a transition from feathers to hair, which occurred largely because hair was more readily available than fancy feathers. Innovative tyers simplified their patterns and began using natural materials such as bear, moose, deer, skunk, and squirrel hair. This was the beginning of the now popular "Rat Series Flies" – patterns such as the Rusty Rat, the Silver Rat, and the Black Rat.

Other traditional yet still popular patterns are: Jock Scott, Dusty Miller, Black Dose, Green Highlander, the Cosseboom Series, Hairy Mary, Blue Charm, Shady Lady, Orange Blossom, Ouo'le, Copper Killer, the Buck Bug, and the Green Machine. The list goes on and on.

These conventional-type flies are again the more popular, but fishing styles were revolutionized on many of these rivers by Lee Wulff, the famous inventor of flies and spokesman for catch and release. He popularized the use of dry flies and the "portland" or "riffled hitch," which is now fished extensively throughout the Atlantic salmon world. He was also the founder of an extremely select club (founded in Canada) called the "16–20" – the requirement for membership is to catch an Atlantic salmon weighing over 20 lbs on a fly no larger than size 16.

Wulff leaves behind him a rich legacy: not only was he responsible, to a large degree, for beginning alternative methods of fishing, but he also initiated innovative changes in flies and tackle, many of which are unlikely ever to be improved. He pioneered the use of extremely light single-handed rods for salmon fishing which, even with the resurgence in the popularity of double-handed rods, still endures.

Perhaps Wulff's single greatest gift to modern-day salmon fishermen was his delight in experimentation, particularly in the rivers of Canada, which has left us such a wealth of fishing knowledge, which enables us both to learn and to enjoy our fishing more.

ESSENTIAL TRAVEL ITEMS

Weather can change quite abruptly in Canada, so it is important to be prepared. Dress in layers, and bring good-quality raingear (both tops and bottoms). Depending on whether you are fishing out of a canoe or wading, you can make the choice between waders or just a rain suit, and between wellies or boat shoes. If you are wading early or late in the season, neoprenes would probably be a wise choice.

During the middle of the season in high summer, lightweight, breathable Gore-tex chest waders will work well. Flannel shirts, long underwear, extra wool socks, a warm sweater, and a hat with a visor are important items that will cover all weather eventualities. Other essentials to take with you to Canada are polarized sunglasses, a fishing vest with lots of pockets for tackle, a collapsible wading staff, a large supply of insect repellent, high-protection sunscreen, and a travel alarm clock. Also, remember your camera and plenty of film.

ABOVE *One reason for fishing Atlantic salmon is to test your skill against what is potentially the largest fish that be taken on a fly in fresh water. This salmon was released to continue her spawning run.*

FLIES, CLOCKWISE FROM TOP
A *Silver Rat; a Silver Stoat; a Ponoi Green;
a Bomber; a Ponoi Red; and a Muddler.*

Trout Among the Shadows

New Zealand

VERLYN KLINKENBORG

"Wilderness is not a state of being, but a principle of action. Clear water favors neither the angler nor the fish, though the angler thinks otherwise. A big trout is wilder than a small trout, and more demoralizing when spooked. The angler was never a fish, though the trout is always a hunter. A trout expects trouble, though the angler wants sport. A trout in hand is the muscular instant that is always vanishing, taking your life away with it."

Tony Entwistle honks when he spots a harrier hawk. So infrequent are cars in this part of New Zealand that harrier hawks rise slowly from road kills, sluggish with possum flesh, fenders brushing their wing tips. Tony and I are driving toward trout-fishing through the top of the South Island. We may go up the Wairau River, a wavering boulevard of parched light that frays across a gravel bed two miles wide. We may ascend the Buller, which runs strong as sin down to the green Buller Gorge from Lake Rotoiti. We may wade in one of a dozen quieter valleys where dark beechen brush climbs from the granite flanks of a small river. We may end up catching fish on the cusp of a hill ripe with sheep.

Near Murchison, the land flattens into a short plain of houses and a street of level shop awnings that lend the town an Old West tang. (We are not far, in fact, from the site of an early New Zealand gold rush.) One buys one's sheep and stud needs at the Murchison Dairy Cooperative, down a dusty avenue, as well as the green slouch hat that Kiwi farmers wear in the rain and sun. (Jaws, necks, hands, and knees burned red, they stand in olive shorts with a pair of dogs at their boots, waving between the poplars as we pass, knowing Tony's car from half a mile away.) Paddocks with orange electric fences and shearing sheds yield instead to sparse yards. On an island in the Buller behind the agricultural arena, a herd of puritanical, nervous-lipped goats, thins blackberry and gorse. Along a side street is the house where Sharon, Tony's wife, was raised, across from a public building now crumbling into stucco rust. No one goes to Murchison to look at Murchison. It tails out soon in the late summer air, which already carries a fall breeze. The mountains steal the eyes away and lift the town apart.

BELOW *Sight fishing for big trout is the name of the New Zealand game. The trout are extremely wary here, so caution and stealth are paramount qualities when trying to catch them.*

Tony and I settle on a river not far distant. We hike on the edge of primal bush, birds ringing like triangles in the branches. We can hear the stream, and we can feel the influence of its freshness in the botanical mist. Darkness condenses around us until Tony, ten paces ahead of me, steps to the

curtain of leaves and parts it, as he has been doing for some time now. This time he stops, and I look, too. A still pool in the river looks back, an eye with life on its surface, life in its depth. I am learning to see the trout Tony finds so cannily for me. What I see is a dark pulse kiting in water the color of twilight air. I backtrack and slither down the bank forty feet behind the pool. Now and again a lens of still water passes over the current, and through it I see a tail, a flash, the cotton mouth. Mostly I notice only shadow, a rock that snakes, a snaking stone with more longitude than latitude. So, like anyone, I cast to it. And it turns out to be a nine-pound brown trout.

RIGHT
A Greenwell's Parachute.

BELOW
A Grasshopper.

Tony watches from high on the bank. We have our arrangements. A leaping nine-pound brown trout is the signal to bring a big net to the water's edge.

Apply your imagination to New Zealand. Think of it as it was in the mid-nineteenth century, when trout were not yet present, when Thomas Brunner and Kehu, his Maori sidekick, were still exploring the Buller Gorge. (They cut trail for 550 days.) The steelhead strain of rainbows would come in ships from California, the browns from England and Tasmania. But before the trout eggs packed on damp moss arrived, those hundreds of rivers, those ribbons of water so clear they look like air on the rocks, were (and still are) inhabited by eels, short-finned and long-finned, black eels the size of a dancer's leg but with teeth where the toes should be. Without the trout, this would be a story about the finest eel-spearing in the world.

If you had seen New Zealand with an angler's eye even then, you would have recognized its unbounded trout-carrying capacity. Imports take well to New Zealand, whether they are fish, timber (rows of furled plywood scroll evenly across the country), or rabbits, which by millions sap high-desert sheep stations, till foremen are forced to gather the shepherds for motorized night shoots week after week. The Kiwis could live with-

RIGHT *A Sawyer's Killer Bug.*

LEFT *A Pheasant-tail Bead Head Nymph.*

out rabbits and thrive without Douglas fir. But the trout simply should have been native; it was an oversight in the Overall Plan.

Not until you get up in the sky does the magnitude of New Zealand's fishing potential really strike you. Streams flow down the knuckles of every wooded hill on the North Island. Like lions' spines, arid mountains ridge the South Island, and from them flow streams as well. Spring creeks, rocky burns, meadow rills, canyon chutes, glacial rivers that lace the desert – the country

is veined and capillaried with water, almost all of it holding trout. Lakes are tentacled with inlets to which trout return to spawn so thickly, say the guides, that you could ford on their backs. Desire mingles with something else on these airborne excursions. You cross a wooded col (trees camouflaging an igneous outcrop) and take a thirty-foot body punch as wind slams the aircraft. The closer you get, the more the urge rises. Along the landscape lies the river, a bracelet of emeralds on a silver chain. "Screw the wind," you think. "Set this baby down so I can fish."

The pilot obliges. He chooses a crease in the hills, choppers groundward, grinning, through a slit in the trees, and on the stream's rubble, disgorges a party of wader-clad anglers (all as rattled as cattle in a cyclone). You feel like badly armed troops, like backyard astronauts in a Martian dust storm. Then the thunder and wind disappear, and the morning composes itself again. A sheath of cool air covers the water. You walk downstream to a pool showing every shade of green through which light can shine, where blowflies drowse on the sand, and foliage tumbles in a slow cascade to the canyon floor. The opaque oblongs in the pool are trout.

That is when you learn, if you have any sense at all, that fishing in New Zealand demands adaption. You realize that you have never seen clear water. Never seen trout this big or this wild. And so you listen carefully to your guide. What you learn by listening is how the game is played at its highest pitch. It is not the game most fly-fishermen know.

In America, insect life is so abundant that our few wild trout have learned to tolerate the presence of anglers by becoming finicky eaters. They push the casserole under their plates, feed the liver to the dog, and confine themselves to Tater Tots. The difficulty of the American game lies in choosing the right fly and making a natural presentation. The rest is peripheral. It can, some days, be golf on water.

But in New Zealand, trout commit suicide in the presence of anglers: they stop feeding. Better to shun calories, they conclude, than get snugged on the nose and lose faith in food. Or they ghost out of casting range, becoming visible to Americans only in the moment they flee. Such wildness adds depth to the game. It creates a Robinson Crusoe effect: if you find fresh footprints along a river, you go home and sulk (or seek another spot). Only rarely do you fish the water blindly.

LEFT Morning mist rises from a pond on the South Island. New Zealand has few trout per mile of river, but the ones that are there are big. You need to spot them before they see you.

ABOVE This is Mitre Peak in Fjordland National Park, one of the wettest areas of New Zealand. I camped in my car overnight to catch first light on the peaks. It was cold and there were sand flies, but the absolute beauty of the morning made it all worthwhile.

123

ABOVE *Local guides are invaluable as they know the country and the flies to use, but most importantly they can spot the fish which are perfectly camouflaged among the rocks on the river bottom.*

ABOVE *Susan Rockrise with a very nice brown trout in the net. Our friend and guide, Norman Marsh, looks happy too!*

Instead, you stalk with great care in dim colors – pausing often to look for that long, pulsing rock on the bottom – or else you lose even the chance to cast. You eschew the vivid fly lines American makers favor (dye one dark olive instead), or in casting you lose the chance to touch the fish – the one going *pfffft!* in the corner of your eye. You learn a heron's stealth.

You also learn a heron's patience. Because New Zealand trout are bigger but more sparsely scattered than the American kind, you hike a long way through willows whose roots turn the shallows pink, through flax plants the size of hyper-trophied yucca, through tussock grass that looks from across the valley like flocks of long-fleeced goats being herded by the wind, through cutty grass that grows in knee-jolting hummocks and bites the hand that grabs it, through ankle-deep jungle moss (and always with a nine-foot fly rod in your fingers), just so you can part the vegetation, peer into the stream, and see a trout as big as any you have ever seen feinting like a boxer. What a miracle of concentration that sight imposes!

Having stalked the fish, you play the American game again. You choose the right fly and make a natural presentation, not so easy after all, because most of the time it means casting a weighted nymph directly upstream. Not far out of Murchison, a glassy little river

LEFT *Sighting, casting, and hooking are the first challenges. Landing is another. The trout are very strong and head for their "hidy holes" right away.*

called the Owen flows down from limestone mountains to the north. Imagine me wet-wading it up to my keister. There is a light haze in the sky, and a kind of amber on the day. Tony, who gets to keep dry because of his good Kiwi eyes, is high on the bluff again, where it is easier to spot fish. I cast twice to a trout, then once to Tony, who catches the fly and changes it. (Tony says, "Trout count to three." The third time they see the same fly, they go *pfffft!*) We do this nine times, a different nymph each one. The keister gets cold. But then, as happens with New Zealand nymph-fishing, I am unconscious one moment, the next moment stumbling downstream after a seven-pound brown.

RIGHT *Guide and angler work together as a team to spot trout and make the correct presentation. If the fish refuses to take a dry, try a nymph.*

In American angling, the deception – making the sale and suckering the trout – is nearly all. But here it just opens debate: New Zealand trout must be captured, not played. On a North-Island river called the Rangitaiki, which curls through the man-made Kaingaroa Forest (a geometrical wilderness of pines and firs), a rainbow hopped before me, behind me, and forged a very large hook into an arrow, the curve bent out of it. On the Buller, a brown trout turned out of the slack, into the current, and peeled my reel. I started to sidestep downstream and looked to Tony for counsel, who shouted: "*Run!*" Run, that is, over a field of stone medicine balls. With 130 yards of line and backing out, the fish disappeared. On the Maruia, near Murchison, I turned the rod the wrong way for an instant as I sprinted beneath a low branch. When I looked back at my trout, away over there, it seemed as if he had fallen from a cloud.

ABOVE *Virtual solitude on a back country river in the fall, on the South Island.*

Sooner or later you land one, and everybody convenes on the river's edge, you, the guide, the trout coming head-up to the net in a final shower of spray. You free the teeth from the bag, the hook from the jaw. With wet hands holding the fish against the current, you look at what you've caught. In its details (you can almost never see it whole), you glimpse the final appeal of New Zealand angling. A brown trout with quarter-size black spots and pale green fire on the gill-plates and jaws, its tense back alligator-hued. A rainbow as sharp as stainless steel, whose black eyes, surveying the waterline, never catch yours. Fins and tails as broad as your handbreadth but which feather off into membranes of air. Jaws that could stitch the thick of your forearm. These fish are not just big; they are the healthiest, most beautiful trout you have ever touched. You release them, they flood their dive tanks, wriggle once, and are gone.

Some days, drizzle hangs in the trees all day long, and the sheep turn especially rank, their outlines blurred like the souls of rich tourists, rain-slicked turds left like tips in the grass. Some days the pumice dust in the wind tries to snatch at your eyes. But other days the autumn sun hammers down, and a gallery of cows watches you warm your legs in a valley that eats your heart up, a place set with pastures and willows and cabbage trees and a single red-tin-roofed cottage in a maze of corral. A gravel road and the river run in tandem to a vanishing point among low peaks. Hoof-wide sheep trails terrace the grassy slopes. In the bush above, there are bare-earth signs of wild pigs rooting. On the highest cliffs, a knot of feral goats rests too, descendants, some say, of Captain Cook's original crew. Despite the shadows and the season, the river will not let the sun fade. As your pants dry from wading, you draw conclusions:

Wilderness is not a state of being, but a principle of action. Clear water favors neither the angler nor the fish, though the angler thinks otherwise. A big trout is wilder than a small trout, and more demoralizing when spooked. The angler was never a fish, though the trout is always a hunter. A trout expects trouble, though the angler wants sport. A trout in hand is the muscular instant that is always vanishing, taking your life away with it.

Water that rises highest above the sea – the earthliest water – is freshest. Upstream, the river bottom is brighter, stones are sharper, and brush hangs tighter to the banks. Trout head upstream naturally, and anglers, pursuing them, do so too. In New Zealand the room for moving upstream seems nearly infinite. So few steps carry you into wildness, so many pools lie between you and a river's source. Wherever you pause, there is a bend farther upstream deepening to azure. It takes a lifetime of fatigue and some powerful nights to keep you from rounding that corner and the next and the next and the next. It occurs to you – just at the moment you turn back home – that New Zealand is upstream of the rest of the world.

ABOVE *A Humpy*.

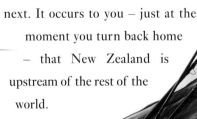

127

NEW ZEALAND – FACTFILE

BACKGROUND

New Zealand is the pearl of South Pacific fishing destinations. This sparsely populated country (approximately 3.5 million people in an area the size of California or the UK) has immensely beautiful terrain. High mountains, thick, virgin forests, lush meadows, and friendly people combine to make this a visiting angler's paradise. New Zealanders, for the most part, live a relaxed, unhurried, pastoral life in the uncrowded countryside; they possess a refreshing wit, and an unmeasured hospitality that beckons and invigorates visitors. New Zealand also gets high marks when measured by the quality of its fishing resources. Both North and South Islands, the country's main land masses, are criss-crossed by rivers and streams that are world famous for their sizeable trout. Rainbows and browns introduced at the turn of the century have taken hold in these waters and represent a major challenge to international fly-fishermen. New Zealand is regarded as the world's greatest trophy trout fishery.

Auckland, the largest urban center, is located on the North Island. The major cities and towns on the South Island are Christchurch, Dunedin, and Blenheim.

WHEN TO GO

Because New Zealand is located in the southern hemisphere, its summer months occur as the northern hemisphere has its winter. July and August are cold and snowy, and Santa Claus comes wearing shorts at the height of summer.

The fishing season opens in October and runs through March. New Zealand's weather is extremely unpredictable. Rain can fall in large amounts and raise the river levels overnight. Indeed, the only criticism one can make of New Zealand is the inconsistent weather. It can and does rain every single month of the fishing season. You simply must accept this and go prepared. New Zealanders often take their summer holiday after Christmas, and the favorite pastime is tramping or hiking, with the result that the countryside is full of local campers during January. Go before or after this time and you will have the fishing pretty much to yourself.

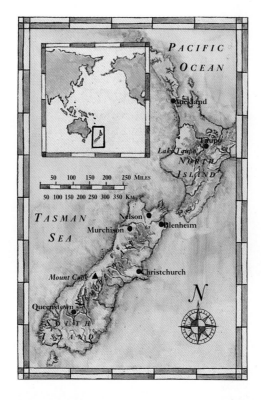

THE FISHING

New Zealand fly-fishing is predominantly sight fishing, meaning that you don't cast until you spot your quarry. This is quality fishing, not necessarily quantity fishing. There may only be a few fish per mile of stream or river here, but the fish that there are will be large – quite possibly the largest trout you're ever going to see. You will spend your time stalking the riverbank cautiously and stealthily until you've spotted a fish (hopefully before he has spotted you). You can present him with a dry fly first, and if he refuses to come up for it, you should switch to a nymph.

New Zealanders are very sophisticated nymph-fishermen. Their method involves casting weighted nymphs, usually in sizes 12 to 15, upstream. Floating lines are used, and the leaders are long (9 to 14 ft) to allow the flies to sink. Regulations permit anglers to use a second nymph tied as a dropper to add weight, but split shot cannot be used on the North Island. As their lines float toward them, the fishermen watch for any slowdown or hitch that looks unnatural.

Engaging the help of one of the local guides is of the utmost importance. Not only do they know the country and the rivers worth fishing, but they know what flies to use and, most importantly, they can spot the fish – which are often very difficult to see – lying camouflaged among the rocks in 6 to 10 ft of water. New Zealand fishing guides have the most unbelievably sharp eyes for spotting fish – this sighting almost becomes a sport of its own.

There are so many rivers in New Zealand that it would take a lifetime to fish them all. Most of them have absolutely crystal-clear water. Both rainbows and browns average 3 to 4 lbs, with 5 lb fish being fairly common. A good day might find an angler and guide spotting a dozen fish and catching five between 4 and 7 lbs. There are quite a few fish reaching weights of double figures to keep you on your toes.

TACKLE

RODS: Graphite rods 9 ft in length for line weights 5, 6, 7, and 8 are recommended for New Zealand fishing. It is a good idea to take several rods – perhaps a 5 wt, a 6 wt, and an 8 wt – for the various weather conditions that you will encounter.

Four-piece travel rods are ideal as you can carry them on the airplane with you for safe keeping. Medium- to fast-action is recommended for accurate casting in windy conditions.

REELS: The freestone rivers of New Zealand are full of slippery rocks. Reels and equipment take a tough beating. Take sturdy, heavy-duty reels that won't bend or break if you should take a fall and bang your reel against a boulder.

All reels should be matched with the appropriate lines for the rods that you are planning to use. A good drag system with 100 yards of backing will do nicely.

LINES: Most of the fishing will be with floating lines, and a weight-forward floating line will work well for long, accurate casts. A sinking-tip line is a good addition. Most New Zealand guides are strong advocates of a dark-colored line that will blend in with the background, and therefore will not spook the fish.

FLIES, CLOCKWISE FROM
TOP LEFT *A Cased Caddis;
a Treacle Parkin; a Royal
Wulff; a Cicada; and a Gold-ribbed Hare's Ear.*

LEFT *Some of the largest brown trout in the world
swim in the rivers and lakes of New Zealand. There
are comparatively few people living on the islands;
the fish have no natural enemies; and every care
possible is taken to ensure that the environment of the
waterways and lakes remains unspoiled by human
hands. As a result, the fish can live a long time here,
and they are able to grow very big: it is not unusual
for brown trout weighing more than 10 lbs to be
caught every season.*

LEADERS: A 9 ft tapered leader with a tippet size of 3X (5 lbs) or 4X (4 lbs) is standard. Take several extra spools of tippet material, as leaders are often changed or broken, and you will almost certainly go rapidly through poundweights of leader material. Take extra spools of 2X (6 lbs), 3X (5 lbs), 4X (4 lbs), 5X (3 lbs).

FLIES: These should be taken to New Zealand in clean, rust-free fly boxes, or preferably in their original containers. Do not take fly-tying material with you, as customs officials carefully watch for materials potentially harmful to New Zealand's agriculture, and fishing equipment that does not look new and clean is suspect.

The universally acclaimed best dry fly in New Zealand is the Royal Wulff (sizes 10, 12, and 14).

Humpies in various different colors are also very popular. The general mayfly imitation is the Adams. Hare's Ears and Pheasant Tails are the number one choice for nymphs. The trout in New Zealand are not nearly as selective as fish in other places, mostly owing to the fact that there is very little fishing pressure. The result is that presentation is just as important as choice of fly.

ESSENTIAL TRAVEL EQUIPMENT

The most important items for a successful fishing trip to New Zealand, aside from tackle, are: good-quality protective raingear (tops and bottoms); a sturdy, wide-brimmed hat to protect you from the sun and to shield your eyes for better vision; yellow-amber-colored polarized glasses for spotting the

trout; and comfortable walking shoes for hiking. Many anglers choose to wade wet during the warm, summer months and wear shorts, with wading boots over socks. As most of the fishing is from the banks, you are usually only in the water long enough to cross the stream. You may also end up walking long distances, and it is much more comfortable to walk in shorts and boots instead of waders. Avoid bright-colored clothing when stalking fish – wear drab colors such as greens and browns to blend in with the surroundings. Don't forget insect repellent. Black flies, no-see-ums, and mosquitoes are often thick just before rain, or at sunrise or sunset. Take a medium-sized day pack or rucksack to carry lunch, raingear, extra wool socks, and so on. The scenery is incredible, so take a camera and twice as much film as you think you'll need.

Jingle Bones

Christmas Island

PETER KAMINSKY

"We started to see the fish in the afternoon. The morning had been hard. We were into the wind on a falling tide. Then we shifted across the lagoons and hit it right. Five fish on five casts.

A cloud darkened the water. We lost sight of the fish. When the sun came out again I watched it light up the flat like a baby's smile. I counted six different colors to the water: white by the shore, then shadowy gray, then copper (from the coral), then light blue followed by green and ending in deep-water blue."

LEFT *A typical view of the one-lane road bordered by palm trees and ocean views. You rarely see any traffic other than trucks driven by fishing guides.*

Ship's Master William Bligh – later of the *Bounty* – spent Christmas Eve 1777 on board *HMS Resolution*, which rode at anchor at the mouth of a lagoon two degrees north of the equator and 160 degrees west of Greenwich, England. In honor of the day, his commanding officer, Captain James Cook, named the surrounding coral atoll Christmas Island.

RIGHT *Purple sea urchins, pushed together by the tides and dried by the sun, lie clustered together by the thousands on some Christmas Island beaches.*

Then, as now, the winter surf piled thirty-foot breakers against the protecting necklace of Cockrane's reef so that the low-lying island (average elevation: five feet) rarely felt the fury of waves that had traveled, unobstructed, across 5,000 miles of open ocean. Cook's journal of the visit betrays few of the rhapsodies that he lavished on Tahiti or the Sandwich Isles, but this is not surprising. Apart from some coconut palms and a scattering of salt bushes, the coral tableland of Christmas Island supports neither fruits nor vegetables, nor any of the game that lives on green things. Cook documented, "Should anyone be so unfortunate as to be accidentally driven upon the island or left there, it is hard to say that he could be able to prolong existence."

On January 1, Cook and Bligh observed the eclipse from their vantage point at the head of the lagoon. Twenty-four hours later the *Resolution* weighed anchor and made for Hawaii.

RIGHT *A fly box, with bonefish and permit flies, positioned among the conch shells, brings back fond memories of the trip.*

ABOVE (FAR LEFT TO RIGHT) *A Yellow Crazy Charlie; a Gray Greg's Flats Fly; a Pink Crazy Charlie; an Orange Snapping Shrimp; a Tan Greg's Flats Fly; a Brown Snapping Shrimp, a Gotcha; a Fuzzy Shrimp; a Spawning Shrimp; a Bonefish Special; a Brown Crazy Charlie; an Eric's Standing Shrimp; a Pink Flash; and a Cave's Shrimp Wobbler.*

I am dead sure that neither Cook nor Bligh was a bonefisherman.

Christmas Island, you see, is blessed with some of the finest, if not *the* finest, bonefishing in the world, which is how and why the following conversation took place in a rusting pickup exactly 207 years, 11 months, and 26 days after Captain Cook's arrival.

"I read that this is the only place in the whole Pacific where you can fish the flats for bonefish, Moana. Why is that?"

"You are wrong," Moana countered. "They have bonefish on Banaba, on Saipan, on many of the atolls. But there are no hotels and too many people who also fish for food. Here we don't eat the bonefish so much."

Moana is the premier fly-rod guide on Christmas Island even though, at the time of writing [1985], he has only been fly-fishing for a little over a year. His full name is Moanafua Tamaika Kofe, which is Gilbertese for "Only-Ocean-Small-Fish-Fishing Pole." Back on his native Tarawa, his father's people have always been fishermen; it is in their blood. His mother's family were warriors; hence his maternal uncle, "He-Who-Carries-His-Enemy's-Head-in-a-Basket."

RIGHT *A view of the sand flats extending as far as the eye can see. Every minute somthing new and unusual happens. The bonefish here are big, hungry, and strong, and will strip out all your backing. Strange fish scurry off the flats in front of you, and the birds are so tame that you can cradle them in your hands.*

On Day One with Moana I caught a fish. On Day Two, both my wife, Melinda, and I caught fish. On Day Three, came the big victory . . . we saw fish! Spotting bonefish is like wingshooting or hitting a baseball; it takes a day or two to get your eye back.

We started to see the fish in the afternoon. The morning had been hard. We were into the wind on a falling tide. Then we shifted across the lagoons and hit it right. Five fish on five casts.

A cloud darkened the water. We lost sight of the fish. When the sun came out again I watched it light up the flat like a baby's smile. I counted six different colors to the water: white by the shore, then shadowy gray, then copper (from the coral), then light blue followed by green and ending in deep-water blue.

Moana pointed to a big one. I tried, but three casts sent him back out to blue water. I moved on. Five minutes later Moana had the fish on. Five minutes after that he had him in, neat, clean, and quick. Twelve pounds.

"We catch bigger ones on the full moon. They return from spawning every month, and, best I can tell, nobody really knows their habits that well, but Moana operates under that assumption and he catches big bonefish.

"Fish across that flat," he said. "Take your time. Cross the islet and fish the lee. They are big."

The Trade Winds whipped the water and our ten-foot casts caught fish. We crossed the small island. Melinda connected with a school of four-pounders. I saw a larger shadow lurking on the edge of the shallows. I cast. He turned. I stripped. He followed. I paused. He lowered his head. I lifted my rod. It bent.

I palmed the reel and the fish slowed his run. When he stopped I pulled back on the rod just above the trademark. I felt him shake his head. He ran toward me and I recovered all my backing. He knifed left. I lowered my rod, Melinda raised hers, and we exchanged positions (she was still fighting one of the schoolies). Mine was nine pounds and change, the biggest bone I had ever caught. He took a while to revive. Finally, he shook his tail and his silver shape became a green shadow that melted off the reef.

Life was great. Moana was happy. I was happy. Melinda was happy, and the car wouldn't start. This is not a good thing anywhere, but especially on Christmas Island, where it is surprisingly easy to get lost and less easy to get found.

Moana covered the air intake. I hit the pedal. Melinda encouraged us. Moana covered the air intake again. I cranked again, and Melinda encouraged some more, *ad infinitum*, till we got it right. *Pachugga, pachugga.* Our semi-trusty car started.

We crossed Poland Channel, passing two bunkers where the British and Americans had observed their H-Bomb tests in the 1950's and '60's. The car didn't die for good until we were two miles from the hamlet of Banana. To my knowledge there are not, and never have been, any banana plants on the island, but it was named Banana by US soldiers in World War II and the name stuck.

We walked through town. All the houses were stamped out of the same cookie cutter: wooden slats, tin roofs, a catch basin for fresh water: all in all, no more exotic than a row of sharecropper's shacks. In the middle of the road, a young man lay on his back, playing his harmonica. A woman, bathing outdoors, picked up the harmony, her nudity taken as a matter of course by the neighbors.

A 300-pound man wearing the traditional lava-lava skirt *putt-putted* along on his long-suffering motor scooter. As he passed us, the reverse angle revealed his young son sitting behind him, looking no bigger than a postage stamp against his father's enormous back. There are very big men on the island – fearsome-looking with their long hair and gappy teeth, but very friendly, like the truck driver who, along with a buddy, invited us into the cab of his enormous rig.

"Where?" the driver asked.

"The hotel," I said.

"No. Where?" he said.

"What where?" I asked.

"You from where?" he said.

"New York," I said.

"Yes?" he said.

"Yes," I said.

"Me Tarawa," he said.

"Tarawa, yes," I said.

I tried to broaden the dialogue and remarked on the pretty sunset. The driver looked at me uncomprehendingly. My wife pointed to the sun and then made circular motions with her hands and said, "Good."

"Yes," he said.

When we slowed at the hotel, the buddy spoke his first words, "Hotel, yes?"

"Yes," I said.

"Thank you," Melinda said.

"Yes," he said, and waved goodbye.

LEFT *The "ole red Punt:" slow-moving but usually dependable. These are the local boats built to carry fly-fishermen to the outer flats on the island.*

ABOVE *It's hard to believe that the crystal-clear water on the flats could conceal anything, but the bonefish blend in so well that all you can make out, as they ghost across the sea-bed, are their shadows.*

Inside the hotel, the locals watched *The Spy Who Loved Me* on the video recorder, a ritual they repeated with fresh delight each night of our stay. And so civilization came to Christmas Island, and we went to sleep.

I haven't told you about the trevally yet, have I? A trevally is a large jack, not unlike the fish that we call a jack crevalle. However, the Gilbertese have no "c" in their alphabet so "trevally" is as close as they get to crevalle (or, as Captain Cook referred to it, "cavally").

If you want to catch a world record fish on a fly, I think two weeks of serious trevally hunting on Christmas Island may reward your quest. These predators often travel in pairs and they will swoop into the flats with breathtaking speed and disappear just as quickly. Be prepared with a nine- or ten-weight outfit, a gaudy streamer, and sixty-pound shock tippet. Once you spot them, you run along the shore as fast as you can, trying to get ahead of them. Lead them with your cast. Strip fast. Rip the water with your line. Make a commotion. They will charge your fly. When they do, let them take before you strike.

I am quite sure I had a shot at a record fish every day, and every one gave me buck fever. I did manage to hook one biggie, but I take no credit for it. I had a small bonefish on. Two trevally came over the reef straight for my fish. They were going

so fast that they overshot on the first pass. One of them swirled, took my bonefish, and headed for open water. The tug felt great. So did the bend in the rod, the zing of the reel, the length of the run. I palmed down on the drag and broke off before he spooled me.

I recall the return drive to camp, feeling about as whipped as a person can be – sun-baked, thirst-crazed, and dog-tired – thinking only of a cocktail, maybe a handful of peanuts, and 36 straight hours of sleep. No sooner had Moana screamed "*Trevally*!!" than I sprang out of the truck like an Israeli commando.

Trevally will sometimes pen up the baitfish and then stun them or cut them in half with a savage flick of their tail. It is a crisp sound: furious and exciting. Twice we cast to such fish: the first time I had to drill my loop through a swarm of man-of-war birds who mistook my lure for a fish. Actually I didn't feel that we were casting to fish. Shadows would be a better word, and everyone knows that you can't catch a shadow.

When the trevally departed, they left a mud swirl ten feet across. We held our breaths and looked for them to come in again. Moana walked into the water and began splashing, a tactic that can attract trevally, which take the splashing for a fish in distress. It made good scientific sense, but seeing him there at sunset, kicking and

ABOVE *A happy angler displays a nice bonefish – almost as big as his smile!*

139

ABOVE *The thatched-roof bungalows of the Captain Cook Hotel silhouetted against the morning sunrise. Ventilated for the constant trade winds, the rooms make sleeping easy and deep in the warm salt air, dreaming to the sound of the surf.*

watching and waiting. I thought for a minute that this was how his ancestors did it, some Micronesian sea magic that put a spell on the water and called the giant trevally to their deaths.

That was Christmas Eve. We made a pact to forego the festivities on Christmas Day. The fishing would be our Christmas. This did not go down well with our hotel mates, who were hoping to form a contingent to attend the singing contest down in the village of London.

"Fishing on Christmas? Are you out of your mind?"

"Where's your Christmas spirit? For God's sake, man!"

"Do you have any idea what kind of a once-in-a-lifetime event you'll miss?"

"Boy! What total jerks!"

Alas, there was nothing I could say. They were right.

Nonetheless, I wanted to fish. Truth to tell, I would rather fish than do anything. No doubt there are some of you out there who feel as I do, so you understand. As it turned out, we all got very drunk that night, which seemed to be the main activity up and down the length of the atoll. When we didn't roll out of bed until ten we decided, "What the heck? Let's go see Christmas on Christmas."

The entire population had camped out in London, the island's largest town. As befits its metropolitan status, it has a jail, a boatyard, a fire engine, a place where you can buy warm beer, and two tin-roofed open-air public meeting houses (each about the size of a basketball court). The dwellings are of the same minimalist design that we had observed in Banana.

Inside the Anglican Church (ladies on one side, men on the other, and please remove your shoes), the priest wore a white lava-lava, a white shirt, and a black tie. The ladies' bright dresses were of a cloth so sheer that you were surely meant to see that every woman on the island wore a brassière. Was this some extra show of propriety to prove that they had forsaken the pagan toplessness of yesteryear?

ABOVE *The local Kiribati people are friendly, and eager to share their culture with visitors. They love dancing and singing.*

We were invited to lunch following the service. We passed among the families camped within the perimeter of the meeting house. Their supplies of fish, meat, and coconut products filled the cupboards that are left there for the convenience of guests. Fathers slept. Babies cried. Teenagers flirted. A rectangle of pillars formed the inner support of the house, and a village elder sat against each pillar. As guests, and according to ancient custom, we were treated like elders.

Like modern vacationers, island people are used to traveling long distances. They think of the entire Pacific the way you think of your county. Still, they don't underestimate the rigors of travel. After all, they used to do it in canoes.

The village teenagers served us a great feast of pork, fish, curried octopus, and pandanus leaf chutney. The elders rolled cigarettes, using the paraphernalia they carried in their handbags. One after another they rose to deliver a benediction that touched on the miracle of Christmas and the importance of our arrival, treating each with equal weight.

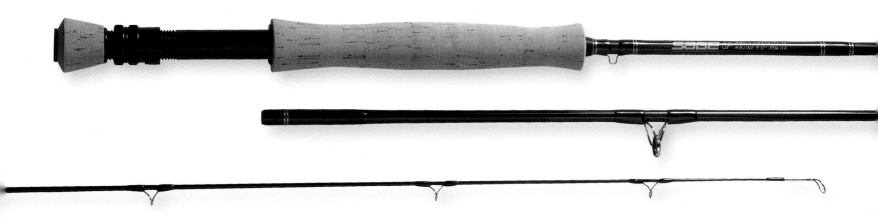

Then the singing began, the yearly contest between the villages of Banana, London, and Poland. Each village had its own uniform: intensely colored lava-lavas, beautiful bright shirts, and flower leis, wristlets, and hair ornaments. They sang Church of England hymns in Gilbertese. The four-part island harmony reverberated off the tin roof of the long house. I found myself on the brink of tears, neither of sadness nor of joy. I was just overwhelmed by the day, the place, the song, and the people.

Still, there were fish out there to be caught. I asked Moana how we could leave without looking ingrates. He told me to give the head elder a donation for the church. I did so in the understated (or is it embarrassed?) way that we "civilized" folk deal with money. Melinda and I rose to leave. The head elder rose with us. He began to speak in a loud voice as he waved our ten dollar bill. I was caught off guard. With great sweeping gestures and trumpeting declamation, he informed the multitude and rejoiced that we had journeyed 10,000 miles so that we might make

RIGHT *The Crazy Charlie is the most popular bonefish fly and is tied in many colors and sizes. No fly box would be complete without a wide selection.*

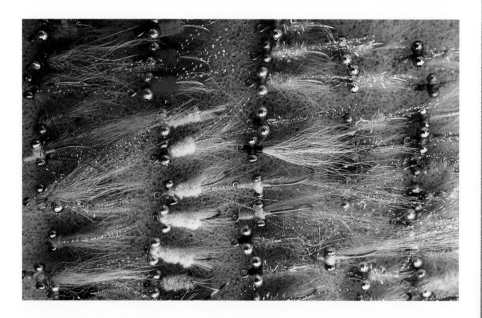

this donation to the well-being of their Church and that this was indeed one of History's Great Events. We blushed at the translation. When the old man finished, he waved the bill again, and in unison every man, woman, and child clapped their hands three times and shouted good wishes to us.

I know an exit line when I hear one.

Melinda and I blew them all a kiss and told them we would never forget them (which we won't). Moana put the pedal down and we rushed to catch the tide on Nine Mile Flat.

"There are five kinds of swimming bonefish," Moana said, apropos of nothing except wanting to make sure that he had told me all he could tell. I took it as his Christmas present.

"One type of swimming bonefish, he spooks at your cast but he doesn't run. Cast again and strip. He will follow. Another kind of swimming bonefish, he just swims along the coast for a mile. You follow him because he will stop. When he stops, he tails and when he tails, you catch him. The third kind is suspended in the current of the tide. He is easy. Cast four feet ahead of him and strip fast. He will strike from the side. The fourth kind he swims in a circle of five-feet diameter. This bonefish doesn't spook but you must use lighter tippet."

"And the fifth kind, Moana?"

"Tailing bonefish," he said. "They are the best of all."

The white flat stretched to the horizon. No action yet, so we walked. The water crept over our ankles. We began to see life. Little morays, small sharks, puffer fish.

CENTER *Anglers arrive by punt and prepare to fish the edge of a flat where it drops off into deeper water. That's where the big bones feed.*

LEFT *An outside flat by the reef is a good place to spot trevally (another gamefish which grows quite large), as they swoop along the edges of the flats, on the brink of the open ocean.*

They inched up the flat, following the water. The bones came last. First the small ones, then the big ones, unhurriedly, inexorably. The late afternoon sun caught their tails and fins – nine miles of tailing bonefish.

It isn't how many fish we caught; it was how we caught them that mattered. You pick one you want. You tiptoe into position. Take a half hour if you need it, but do it right. Work him like a rising trout. Cast as many times as necessary. Don't scare him. Strip when his fin disappears. Watch for the take.

Merry Christmas!

CHRISTMAS ISLAND – FACTFILE

BACKGROUND

This tropical destination in the middle of the Pacific ocean, some 1,300 miles south of Hawaii, is part of the Line Island group, in the Republic of Kiribati. Christmas Island has the largest land area of any coral atoll in the world (140 square miles) and is only 119 miles north of the equator. With its large colonies of seabirds, vast reefs, endless flats, lagoons, and surrounding ocean, it offers excellent opportunities to observe bird and marine life, as well as to enjoy outstanding fishing.

The island was discovered by Captain James T. Cook on Christmas Eve in 1777, hence the name. It remained part of Great Britain until 1979, when Kiribati regained its independence. Nowadays, there is a strong Australian influence throughout Christmas Island.

WHEN TO GO

The island enjoys equatorial calm, lying well east of Pacific storm development areas. Because of its proximity to the equator, it does not have seasons as such. The temperatures in January are virtually identical to those in July.

Easterly trade winds blow throughout the year at an average of 10 to 20 knots, and provide a cool breeze across the flat surfaces of the atoll. Out on the flats each day it is rarely humid or unpleasantly hot. The average daytime temperature is around 80°F (28°C), and the evenings cool down to a breezy 72°F (20°C).

Annual rainfall averages 30 inches and is normally in the form of afternoon or evening showers. It is best to be prepared with a light rain jacket in case you get caught in a downpour. There seems to be a 5-year drought cycle, which may be worth investigating.

Cloud cover is relatively sparse throughout the year compared with other tropical areas, and, in general, conditions are ideal for flats fishing. From June to September, the winds tend to be calmer and the sea less rough. Christmas Island certainly seems

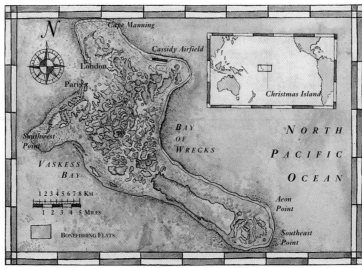

to have the most consistent and predictable sunny weather patterns of any bonefishing destination in the world.

THE FISHING

The island, with its long fishing season and sympathetic climate, is perhaps the single most popular year-round destination for bonefishing, boasting vast numbers of fish – some of them very big – on easily waded, clean, hard, white sand flats. Experienced flats anglers will sometimes average between 15 and 20 bones a day, with a 30-plus fish day possible at any time. While most of these fish may average about 3 to 4 lbs, several could be in the 6 to 9 lbs bracket. Trophy bones are always possible. There have been numerous reports of weighed and measured 10 to 13 lb fish, and even larger fish have been spotted, hooked, and lost – as, of course, is always the case.

Adding to the excitement daily are 3 different kinds of trevally (a type of jack) – giant (up to approximately 100 lbs), blue (up to 15 lbs), and striped (up to 20 lbs or more) – which are taken with fly, although, owing to their fierce fighting ability, they can also be caught on baitcasting or spinning tackle on the flats while you are out bonefishing, as well as along the lagoon edges and in the surf. Trevally are awesomely strong fish that strike savagely at or near the surface.

Virtually all of the bonefishing is by wading. Ninety per cent of the flats are white or yellowish sand, coral marl, or, in a few cases, coral shelves, which can be brownish in color. There is little or no "turtle" grass on any of the flats. Take some care, as there are some soft areas that generally should be avoided: be careful not to wade on the lightest (or whitest) areas, which sometimes have a puffy extruded appearance, or places where there are undulating depressions with burrow holes in the bottom, which will have been made by giant snapping shrimp.

Fishermen are transported to the flats either in light trucks or in lagoon "punts" – large flat-bottomed boats, which are also used for trevally fishing in the protected waters of the lagoon. Guides switch off the engines as they approach the fish, and will gently pole you into the perfect fishing position.

TACKLE

RODS: 9 to 9½ ft graphite rods in 7, 8, or 9 wt are ideal. Beginners and novices may be better off with an 8 wt: the extra backbone will facilitate casting, especially in windy conditions. It is advisable to take more than one rod in case of breakages.

REELS: Those with reliable, smooth, adjustable drags seem to work best. Few fish will stress a reel like a bonefish, so bring sturdy, high-quality models specifically designed for saltwater use. Reels must hold your line and at least 150 yards of 20 to 30 lb Dacron backing.

Although most Christmas Island anglers feel comfortable with direct-drive reels, some fishermen, especially novices, may prefer anti-reverse models. The handles on anti-reverse reels remain stationary when running bonefish pull line off the reel, as opposed to the handles on direct-drive reels, which spin rapidly when fish run – often resulting in bruised knuckles, and even lost fish. Take a spare reel and/or extra spools with you each day so that you can regroup on the flat if you lose a fly line.

LEADERS: Use 9 to 12 ft leaders in the 10 to 15 lb range, and don't forget extra spools of 8, 10, 12, and 15 lb clear tippet material. When fishing, check your leader frequently for wind knots and coral abrasion, and change tippets as often as necessary. The best results have been with stiff, abrasion-resistant leader and tippet material.

FLIES: There are several factors that dictate proper fly selection on Christmas Island. When choosing the color of the fly, it is best to try to match the bottom coloration as closely as possible. If you are fishing on a very light-colored flat, cream or white patterns work best. If the bottom is tan or off-color, then patterns in various shades of brown should be the most productive. The general guideline is to switch colors if you find that you are getting multiple refusals.

In most cases, Christmas Island bones tend to prefer patterns in size 4. If you are fishing in shallow water or where the fish are tailing, try smaller sizes as they can be presented more subtly. The Crazy Charlie is the most commonly used fly on Christmas Island. The guides can tie very acceptable flies and appreciate fishermen buying flies from them. They, of course, know which colors and patterns you are most likely to find successful.

Christmas Island custom encourages fishermen to pinch down the barbs on the hooks of their flies with pliers, as this makes it much easier to release the fish unharmed. Many people feel that the barbless fishing hook actually works better in penetrating the tough tissue of a bonefish's mouth, and, generally, you may catch more fish.

ESSENTIAL TRAVEL EQUIPMENT

Precautions against the sun should be a priority. It is a good idea to have long-sleeved shirts and long pants to tuck into your wading shoes or your socks. To be safe it is advisable to carry high-protection sun cream, which should be applied to all exposed skin, and reapplied every hour while you are outside. Even if you wear a wide-brimmed hat, the sun reflecting off the water will burn your lips and face unless you conscientiously apply sunblock.

As you will spend a lot of time on your feet, it is important to have comfortable wading shoes. Some

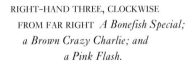

ABOVE Albula vulpes, *or the bonefish as he is more commonly known, is an amazing creature. First you need to see him as he ghosts along the flats. Then you need to catch him – he's as fast as the wind. Few other fish fight as hard, pound for pound. When you hold him, he is as bright as polished silver in the sun.*

people choose ankle-height canvas tennis shoes, one size larger than normal; others use conventional stream wading shoes. Flats booties, available at all large fishing stores, are especially designed for wading the flats.

Take a lightweight cotton fishing vest or shirt with plenty of pocket space. Polarized sunglasses with UV protection are essential. Clippers for cutting monofilament and a waterproof boat bag are also useful items.

FLIES: BOTTOM SIX, CLOCKWISE FROM CENTER *A Cave's Shrimp Wobbler; a Fuzzy Shrimp; a Yellow Crazy Charlie; a Gotcha; a Brown Snapping Shrimp.* TOP FIVE, CLOCKWISE FROM TOP *A Pink Crazy Charlie; an Eric's Standing Shrimp; a Tan Greg's Flats Fly; an Orange Snapping Shrimp; and a Gray Greg's Flats Fly.*

RIGHT-HAND THREE, CLOCKWISE FROM FAR RIGHT *A Bonefish Special; a Brown Crazy Charlie; and a Pink Flash.*

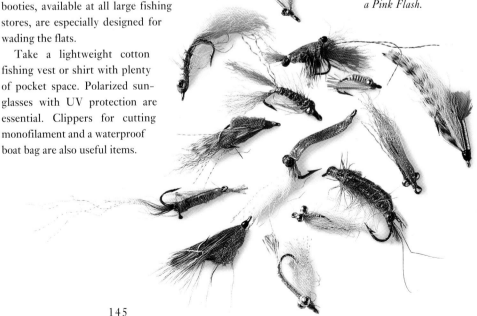

Fly-fishing in the Middle Ages

Russia

DAVID PROFUMO

"Sunlight suddenly lit the pool, and I had a surprising moment of certitude: the deep golden water gargled around my legs, and I felt a familiar, slight effervescence along my lower spine, that presentiment that something is going to happen. Arthur Ransome likened this to those strange occasions when silence descends on a crowded room, and at such moments in Czarist days they used to say, 'a policeman is being born'. To me, it is the 'fishological moment'."

Yesterday I was perched glumly at my desk in London, now I am wading down the Home Pool just below the Ryabaga camp and the water is like velvet in the evening light. We are fishing the "buddy system", and Steve squelches up in his chest-waders: "Hey, Dave, show us that Spey throw again". I raise my rod-tip to go into the first curve of the cast I have been practising, but there comes a pulsing resistance – by luck, my first fish, an hour into the trip. This only happens to other people, in books. We tail out the grilse, and release him. Time for a hit on the Duty Free back in the tent, and then bed. It's been a long journey, but for now I'm Top Rod. I swagger back to the camp as if I were the love-child of Dame Juliana Berners and Zane Grey, the Arctic deities duly recording my hubris.

Murmansk is the world's northernmost metropolis, and the only sizeable city within the Arctic Circle. Famous for salted halibut, it's a tenebrous port of classic Soviet concrete, aptly described by one native guidebook as "situated in a depression" (they say it's not actually twinned with anywhere, but is enjoying a suicide pact with Grimsby). Our chunky old MI-8 chopper judders away on its two-hour flight southeast across the Kola Peninsula, and over the flatlands of the tundra plateau. There has never been systematic agriculture here, and the terrain looks like a huge, jigsawed mossbank, with tracts of water gleaming through the cuts and gouges. It's a desert of scrub and shrub. Perhaps more than any other fishing destination I have glimpsed – the burning bonelands of Christmas Island, or those austral fjörds of the Falklands, included – this aerial overview is essential to an appreciation of the Ponoi River's strangeness.

Its catchment area (6,000 square miles) is both vast and desolate, home to a few semi-nomadic Saami whose reindeer crop the yagel moss. It's an inhospitable prospect: in the winter it can reach –50°C here, and for three months the sun never appears above the horizon, though the darkness during these polar nights is said to be relieved by nocturnal snowgleam and the Northern Lights. It is not even that travel writers' cliché, "a land of contrasts", for its barrenness seems unredeemed until suddenly you sight the great river itself, cutting down through the bedrock, its drainage giving rise to woodlands of spruce and pine along the gorge. Indeed, as it makes its way east towards the Barents Sea, the Ponoi forms the barrier between the tundra zone and a forest region – the taiga lands of spaghnum, birch, willow, cowberry and lichen. And there, below, on its lower shore, is our tented camp, isolated like some improbable moon station.

I have never felt entirely at ease on the Kola Peninsula since that "white night" in 1990 when I heard the wild women singing.

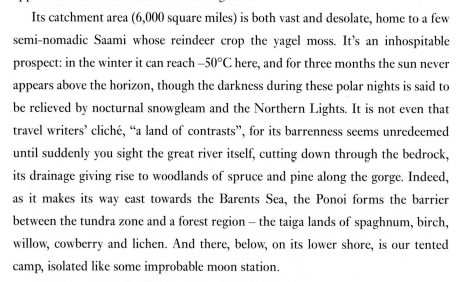

That was on an exploratory trip to the Middle Umba (another mighty river, to the southwest) during July, a month up here characterised by two phenomena: the bug season (despite thirty summers' exposure to the Scottish midge, my body erupted like the Elephant Man's), and the Arctic day, which means the sun never quite sets ("white nights"). Around three in the morning I was an hour's trek from camp, fishing an area of islands where the river split into an isthmus of five streams above a lake, when I heard female voices singing on the wind. We were fifty miles from any town, and there are no roads; a few male poachers lurk in the woods, scarcely the raw material for an ethereal choir. I could not make out any words, and nor could my companion – a brusque Yorkshireman, not given to flights of fancy, who had waded out of the run to stand beside me.

The singing lasted for maybe ten minutes, after which we decided to call it a day (night). It might have been caused by mozzie toxin, but I don't think so: in former times, tribes returned each year to such places to reap the short harvest of the salmon runs, and I believe what we heard were some of their habitual songs of that season, left behind in the air.

There is evidence that by the middle of the sixth millennium BC small groups of hunting and fishing nomads migrated to this area from the Baltic, when the peninsula was covered in timber (bogs appeared once the climate warmed up, in the Atlantic period). Though sparse, the "Kola culture" of late Neolithic times shows bone implements (there was no flint) and basic burial systems involving fish-scales and -skeletons. By the Bronze Age these settlers were seafaring, and hunting

ABOVE LEFT *Helicopters parked near the Ponoi River camp stand in readiness for another day of flying guests out to remote locations.*

ABOVE RIGHT *An early camp picture, from the "old days". The evening campfire became the magnet for friendship and merrymaking.*

elk and wild bull. In places – fresh or salt – where fish were to be found abundantly in season, spiral labyrinths of granite were arranged on the shoreline, some of them forty feet across. Such intricacy suggests a ritualistic purpose.

Excavations have revealed amber carvings of animals and fish, plus other zoomorphic figures in scattered sites: but then this culture apparently disappears, about 500 years before the birth of Christ.

The Umba had proved to be a dud, but my week on the Ponoi might have altered my entire perspective on salmon fishing. Of the forty or so rivers I've tried for Atlantics it was the most action-packed place I've ever wet a hook – and, to avoid brochurism and superlatives, I'd rather define it in terms of how it differed from my usual experiences of salmon fishing.

Most of my gamefishing is done in the British Isles and Ireland: for a start, we don't generally have sporting camps like this, where strangers commingle for a week or more. Our inns and hotels foster quite different group dynamics – doubtless weird to foreign visitors – but companionship is a crucial part of fishing, and I was lucky at Ryabaga to team up with Robert and Alistair, two expat Brits from Connecticut. My new friends were both energetic and experienced (Alistair had an incredible Alta salmon of 54 pounds on fly to his credit) and the triumvirate had its first day out on the Lower Tomba beat, guided by Jeff Vermillion. The river was a little high to be in perfect ply, but the guides were all positive and resourceful – this was the first difference for me, after decades of gillies, and the professional gloom of Celt or Gael. I lost a good, bright fish in the first pool we tried, after ten minutes struggling to bring it near the gravel bar along which I had waded, and it seemed virtually all day Jeff put us over fish. I was not used to this, either.

Long ago – and I can still picture the little Hebridean lodge where I came to this conclusion – I decided that arithmetic and salmon angling don't mix, and the man who is constantly hung up about the number of fish he has caught is really a guy anxious about his masculinity. Still, one can hardly describe a river like the Ponoi and avoid all mention of numbers. Between the three of us we played 24 salmon that day, and this was not considered a bonanza. The last one I had took me on the dangle, and, though I am quite hard on fish and tend to use stout tackle, it was almost twenty minutes before I brought her in – a silver darling of sixteen pounds, with that lavender sheen to her flanks, and for a moment all mine.

"Ain't it a neat river, though?" grinned Jeff, lighting his end-of-session smoke. I felt as triumphant as the champion crab-catcher of Kamchatka.

That night a bunch of us sat up late in the dining tent, sipping Stolichnaya, regaled by piscatory tales from Pierre (a French guest whose partner in life, Elaine, was a glamorous black jazz singer – a *rara avis* in this neck of the woods), and he told us of his experiences dry fly-fishing for crocodiles, using a live chicken. Before the Stolly stole all the remaining sense out of my ballpoint, I slunk to my tent to jot down initial impressions of this exceptional place.

With no licensed nets or poaching, and zero pollution, the Ponoi is frankly a privilege to fish in the modern age: the first twelve days of the season had rewarded anglers from the camp with almost 2,000 salmon. That would be a decade's tally from many of the rivers featuring in my fishing log. At times the runs are so prolific it gives one a rare glimpse of how things once were elsewhere: it's like fly-fishing in the Middle Ages.

ABOVE *One of the best pools on the Ponoi is the Home Pool, located only a hundred yards from camp. Anglers often visit it for a few casts after dinner.*

ABOVE *A panorama of the Ponoi River camp showing the tents, the river, and the vast wilderness beyond.*

The biggest of the region's 65 salmon rivers, the Ponoi may not be quite as torrential as some of its northern counterparts, but it can present a daunting prospect. At a hundred yards across, it's large even by our Tay standards, and the trick is to discern the distinct streams within the watercourse, and concentrate accordingly; whilst there is often some truth in the Spanish maxim *a rio revuelto, ganancia de pescadores* (meaning "in the troubled stream, gain for the fishermen"), aggressive wading is not always the key to more strikes, and it is possible to overcast certain lies. Subtle strategies learned on smaller rivers can occasionally pay off here.

Mind you, with several miles of water at your disposal each day the average British angler – used to trying the same pools all week – will also feel spoiled for choice. It's pleasantly hard work covering your beat, clambering in and out of the boat and then wading your way amid the rocks, hour after hour, but you just fish through, for all you are worth – "Ride straight, and ride like hell", as the pig-stickers of the Raj used to advise newcomers to their peculiar pastime.

A word about "catch and release" (or *prise et remise*, as it is more stylishly known in Canada): many of us have been voluntarily practising this with salmon in certain

UK rivers for years, but it has to be said that the whole notion of "borrowing" a salmonid has not yet leached into the mainstream of our sport. The majority of our anglers kill salmon, if in good condition, and eat them. This was the tradition in which I was brought up – historically, it used to have something to do with private ownership of fishing rights – and I have to say there persists for me a palpable difference in terms of passionate chemistry between losing near the net a fish you were anyway bound to release, and parting company just before the *moment critique* with one you might have decided to keep.

No doubt suitably funded philosophers are resolving this enigma as we sleep.

With virtually all our salmon waters privately husbanded and preserved, the British angler today enjoys little in the way of true wilderness experience. Most of our pools are particularised with names, and at least a hundred years of oral

153

RIGHT *A fancy wooden box containing some beautiful flies – the question is, which one to use?*

RIGHT *A fancy wooden box containing some beautiful flies – the question is, which one to use?*

ABOVE *A Thunder and Lightning.*

ABOVE *A Durham Ranger.*

history: the beat on the Tweed that I fish each autumn not only has fabled casts but individual rocks recorded in Victorian literature. By contrast, the Kola Peninsula was closed for military reasons until 1989, so its stones are as yet unstoried and its liquid mythology is still in the making.

The unwary European, used to footpaths along his beat, and bankside huts with soft furnishings (on the Tay there's rumoured to be one boasting a chandelier), might find all this wilderness occasionally overwhelming. Personally, I appreciate the joys of solitude: but I do recall a moment, wading deep around some dinosaur boulders at the mouth of the Pornache tributary, when I stepped into a dip where the stream churned below the rocks, and I realised I couldn't retreat. The rest of the party had boated away out of sight, and I felt a deep jolt of loneliness. (I was drying off on the bank, when they returned.)

The Ponoi salmon seem to behave more wildly, too. This may be because they are closer to their marine feeding grounds (I don't know), but they frequently charge the fly with a gusto rare on my home waters: sometimes the same fish will come three or four times before making up its mind, and the takes can be volcanic. If the temperatures are right, they also show well to a Muddler or dry fly; as a result, for every fish landed you probably enjoy some form of reaction from about four others. Except in fortuitous circumstances – such as a concentration of grilse briefly stopping in a pool, or a shoal of salmon entering a loch after a drought – this sort of sport no longer exists in Britain.

LEFT *Late August, and the beginning of fall, can put color in the leaves and frost on the rod rack.*

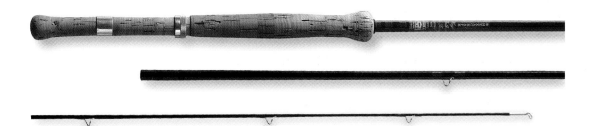

In the modern period, man has altered the weather and broken the wheel of the seasons. Many of the great migrations that used to articulate the year – bison, pigeon, even aquatic insects themselves – have become a thing of the past, and the runs of Atlantic salmon have been extinguished from hundreds of Europe's water-ways. I am wary of nostalgia, but sometimes I stand on the banks of my local river, the Thames (which I have fished since I was a schoolboy), and imagine what England's ancient artery must have been like in its piscatorial heyday.

Legend has it that on the eve of the consecration of London's first church (in 616), St Peter himself promised good salmon fishing for ever to a ferryman and his family, provided they offered a tenth of all catches to the church – and records suggest that the Thames was for centuries a commercially viable fishery, with a healthy run of salmon. Hard up after the crusades, for example, Richard I sold off the salmon-netting rights to the City Corporation in 1197 for the measly sum of 1,500 marks – one of the first concessions of the sovereign's supreme prerogative in all English history. Shortly thereafter, Henry III began his menagerie in the Tower, and the king of Norway gave him a polar bear which was swum daily in the river on collar and leash, to catch salmon for its supper.

When I get my hands on that time machine, I shall take my Thomas & Thomas double-hander back to the medieval Thames, and start in just below the bridge.

The myth persists – though documentary corroboration is lacking – that at this period apprentices in London and elsewhere had inserted into their indentures an article specifying they should not be fed salmon more than once a week. This gives some idea of how common the fish once were, though I think the real reason was that leprosy was thought to be brought on by eating fish.

Right up until Regency times, professional fishermen on the Thames sent some 3,000 salmon to Billingsgate each season. Nemesis came with the discharge from gasworks, sewage, the building of pound-locks to make the river navigable, and greed. There have been recent efforts to re-salmonise the river, but whether the fish can reproduce is uncertain. George IV is said to have bought the last truly wild Thames salmon in 1820 for a guinea a pound, from a fisherman named Finmore.

By the Thursday, I had hooked more salmon in a week than I would normally encounter in a season, but the Kola gods had not forgotten my earlier arrogance.

We went downstream to Hard Curve – a stunning flight, only four metres above the water – and guide Rick said we just might be in for a bonanza; there had been a high tide and a full moon the previous day, and the first of the autumn fish were due any time (this was early September). Like a fool, I counted my chickens.

Back at the dock that evening there were general reports of a good day: one guy had landed a 23-pounder (a large fish for this system); our party had taken seven. "Hell, today I guess everyone caught a buncha fish," smiled Jack, a judge from Louisiana, who looked as if he were going to order me to get a haircut. I mumbled something polite. But I was the only person in camp who had caught nothing.

Slouching off to sulk alone in the sauna with the last of my whisky, I felt the black dog of despair snapping at my heels. I had fished badly that day, and I knew it – I'd missed the few offers that came my way, and my concentration had melted. Every cast should have an idea behind it, but by the afternoon I had become mechanical, resentful, hopeless. In psychic terms, the difference between no fish and one fish has got to be one of the greatest distances in the universe. And tomorrow was my last chance. Half-man half-scotch, I lumbered back to my tent in the dark like some beast of the Apocalypse.

Next day began with a roasting great hangover. It felt as if my mouth had been used as a pottery kiln all night, but I made it through breakfast and by the time the

ABOVE *Standing on a hillside, after dinner, I shot this picture of the camp. Its lights glow in the lingering twilight of one of summer's "white nights."*

boat had roared down to Gold Creek my crapula had been ventilated by the Arctic ozone. I had the beat to myself, as the others were fishing lower down, and I rolled a bright fish in the twisting water at the tail of our first run. He would not come again, but Dima my guide felt we were in business: "Maybe next pool is good, Dave," he said levelly, as he dropped the boat. I needed to believe him.

Wading in at the neck of the fast stream, I lengthened some line and made a goodish cast square across the current. Sunlight suddenly lit the pool, and I had a surprising moment of certitude: the deep golden water gargled around my legs, and I felt a familiar, slight effervescence along my lower spine, that presentiment that something is going to happen. Arthur Ransome likened this to those strange occasions when silence descends on a crowded room, and at such moments in Czarist days they used to say, "a policeman is being born". To me, it is the "fishological moment".

My Willie Gunn began to track round in an arc, and a fish flared off its lie and surged at it: in my excitement, I struck hard – and, against all the rules, this hooked it. That salmon did not come off, nor did the next five (I even had a brace of sea trout, as a bonus). "You're certainly making up for your blank day," observed Alistair pointedly into his soup – when we met up for lunch they'd had one apiece, and a smashed rod. We sipped a little Russian cabernet, and fended off looming thoughts of home. But I was still on a roll, and prayed silently to St Zeno – patron saint of fish hooks – that the fish would not all run through, or switch right off.

We swapped beats, but my luck held. At five to six, Dima histrionically consulted his watch. "One more drop," he announced. We had landed nine, and I had never managed double figures in the thirty years since I caught my first salmon.

A fish turned below the cliff, and with the third fly we tried there came a strangely gentle take, but he felt the steel and went into an aerial lambada. He made for the tailwater, and I braked him hard off my Bogdan: that fish weighed twelve pounds – I know, because we kept him for dinner.

They say you can't step into the same river twice, and I don't know if I'll ever make it back to the Ponoi. People ask if the experience of such plenty spoils you for the fishing elsewhere, but it does not. Ever since I caught my first salmon from a modest spate river in the Scottish Highlands – with a spliced greenheart rod and a line of dressed silk – I have become inured to droughts, dearth and disappointment. The opportunities offered by the Ponoi now seem slightly unreal. It was like a harem, but I know my natural place is back in the small-town dancehalls.

RUSSIA – FACTFILE

BACKGROUND

The Ponoi River is located just north of the Arctic Circle, at approximately 67°N. Flowing roughly from west to east, it enters the Barents Sea on the southeast coast of the Kola Peninsula. The river is easily identifiable on any map as it is the largest on the Peninsula.

The Ponoi stretches more than 250 miles in length, originating in a large tundra plateau which acts as a reservoir, tending to neutralize the effects of a sudden fluctuation in water levels. The river varies from 200 ft to more than 500 ft wide, but maintains a gentle gradient and easy flow. There are a number of good tributaries which, like the great Ponoi itself, hold salmon.

WHEN TO GO

This northerly marine climate can be quite variable and fishermen should be prepared for any weather conditions. In early June, the short spring meets summer, and the average temperatures are unpredictable. You can expect occasional rain, with temperatures dipping into the low 40's at night and rising to as high as the 60's at other times.

From late June through the end of July, the Ponoi has its summer weather. Rain is infrequent and the long days heat the tundra – sometimes creating tee-shirt weather. If you do get caught in an unexpected rainshower, or even if you are fishing on a particularly cloudy day, temperatures can fall to the mid-40's. But at the height of summer, daytime temperatures in the 70's and 80's are common, and often anglers find themselves over-clothed.

August is a pivotal month and the weather can be either an extension of the recent summer, or possibly a prelude to the cold storms that turn up during fall. Lower temperatures are brought on by the fall rains, when it can be as cold as the high 30's or, at best, low 40's, particularly during the night.

If you are lucky and you catch the leftover summer, daytime temperatures can still reach into the 60's and 70's.

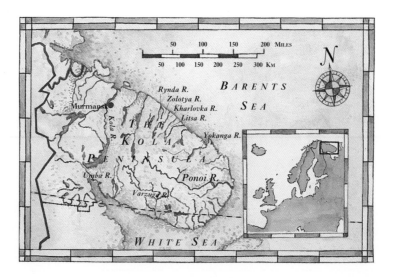

Almost certainly the most harsh weather will arrive with the onset of September. By the time wind and rain from the north have reached the Ponoi, they may have turned to icy gusts and snow, with average daytime temperatures in the mid-30's – they will most likely never exceed the low 50's even if the late summer has been superb. You can expect the temperatures to fall into the 20's at night, so make sure you wrap up warm if you are planning your trip for this time of year.

Throughout these four months, which constitute the short summer season, recorded extremes are from 25°F (–2°C) low to 88°F (30°C) high. Relative humidity is 50 to 80 per cent, and the average monthly rainfall is 2 to 2½ inches spread over 14 to 16 days.

THE FISHING

The Ponoi River is home to salmon that will never even have seen an artificial fly. The river has liberal fishing hours and there are no limits on catch and release. Nevertheless, it is advised that anglers use only barbless hooked flies, and it is especially important to pinch down the barbs when using double-hooked flies – this is one of fishing's untouched idylls, and the river and its unique natural stock levels need to be protected and nurtured so that it can be enjoyed just as it is for many generations to come.

The Ponoi is a large, open river, with pools that are long and wide. Many of these pools can be fished by wading and bank casting, while others are best fished from an anchored boat which is gradually moved through the pool.

TACKLE

RODS: If you use the traditional double-handed rods for 9 to 11 wt line, you may find that this longer rod will make line mending somewhat easier, and will enable you to cast all day without tiring.

Some people prefer single-handed rods, which are light line weight rods – quite acceptable for tributaries and for the size of the salmon typical to the Ponoi. However, we recommend the 9 wt line for casting some of the larger flies used on the main river.

A further consideration in favor of the heavier rod is its ability to fight and land salmon quickly and safely. Whichever rod you choose, a useful addition is a 1½ to 3 inch fighting butt.

The double-handed rod is particularly useful during the early season or during periods of high water, when fishermen are frequently forced to make spey and long-distance casts from the bank or from positions that offer little back-cast room.

REELS: A sturdy reel with reliable drag system is essential for this river. If the reel design includes the added breaking control of an exposed rim, so much the better.

An audible click on the outgoing revolution of the reel is a desirable addition, as it advises your guide as to just what is transpiring between you and your salmon.

The reel of choice should hold the fly line, plus 120 to 175 yards of either 20 or 30 lb backing. Interchangeable spools are nice but not absolutely essential, provided that your tackle supplier rigs your fly lines loop to loop with the backing so they can be easily switched.

LINES: Atlantic salmon on the Ponoi River respond best to a relatively high-riding fly. For this reason, floating, intermediate-density fly lines, have been the favorite on the river to date. There are some pools that dictate the use of a sinking-tip fly line, and so you may be wise to include one.

The Ponoi is a perfect place for those anglers who are familiar with shooting heads. There is ample casting room on most pools; and some lies require a cast 60 ft and up, an easier distance to cast with a double-handed rod or a shooting head. Again, loop to loop facilitates tip changes.

The ideal combination is a floating or running line with a 6 to 8 inch loop that attaches to your 30 to 40 ft tips. 20 lb Dacron backing is sufficient. Splices should be smooth and knot-free.

You may find the intermediate fly line particularly useful in June, followed by a high-floating dry line. Floating-line fishing will be most common July through September, although the sinking-tips should be a part of your kit anytime in case of high water. A sinking-tip fly line or a sinking line should also be included, though at times they can be harder to fish in the more boulder-strewn pools. It is also useful to have a small container of fly line dressing.

LEADERS: A tried-and-tested leader is 7½ to 9 ft of 8 to 15 lb tippet strength, with a butt section that is stiff enough to turn over a 1/0 salmon fly. A dozen knotless 10 lb leaders should be sufficient, along with a good supply of tippet material in a variety of sizes ranging from 8 to 16 lb test. An 18 inch butt of hard nylon attached to the tip of each fly line may also prove a successful pointer. A small perfection loop in the tip of this butt will speed the changing of your leaders.

FLIES: The water of the Ponoi River, though clear, has a brownish color. So, for those anglers who like to match their leader colors to that of the water, flies that are made of red- or brown-colored materials will blend best with the water.

ESSENTIAL TRAVEL EQUIPMENT

A layered approach to clothing is best in this region so that you can add or subtract layers as needed. Long johns are a good idea under your neoprene waders; take plenty of cotton shirts to wear beneath flannel shirts or fleeces, and lots of sweaters.

Take a waterproof fishing jacket with plenty of pockets for tackle. Fishing pants made of cotton or canvas, which will dry quickly and can provide a valuable extra layer or are cool when worn alone, are perfect. If you are going when the weather is likely to be warm you might want to pack a pair of shorts.

Rubber-soled shoes and thermal fingerless gloves are perfect for this area. Polarized sunglasses with UV protection should be standard.

If you are particularly sensitive to insect bites, take plenty of repellent with you. You may even want to wear a head net at times, though most of the insects have usually disappeared by the middle of August.

FLIES: LEFT-HAND SIX, CLOCKWISE FROM TOP *A Yellow Ally's Shrimp; a Willie Gunn variant; an Ally's Shrimp; a Thunder and Lightning variant; a Bomber; and a Thunder and Lightning.* RIGHT-HAND SIX, CLOCKWISE FROM TOP *A Copper Shrimp; a Willie Gunn; a Munroe Killer; a Mickey Finn; a Silver Rat; and a Comally.*

ABOVE *The Atlantic salmon runs up the Ponoi River continue to amaze visiting anglers with the sheer numbers of fish. This river, located far from the "madding crowd," in virgin country, represents a good example of what things used to be like in the old days.*

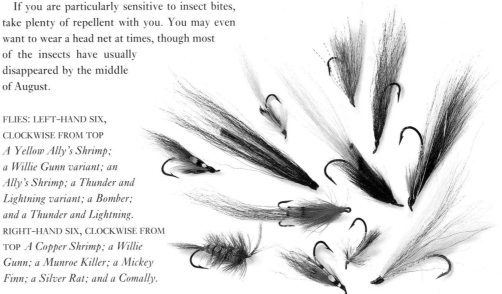

Sons

Mexico

TOM McGUANE

"We were actually fishing in the middle of the Sian Ka'an biosphere reserve – over a million acres of the coast of Quintana Roo, savannas, lagoons, seasonally flooded forest. Our camp, a simple comfortable place for fishermen called Casa Blanca, meets the Mexican requirement of integrating human use with preserving the complex and delicate local ecosystem whose uniqueness derives not only from the phenomenon of a tropic sea inundating a vast limestone shelf, but from long human history."

ABOVE *If you can tear yourself away from the fishing, there are many famous Mayan ruins to explore in the Yucatán, including Uxmal, shown here.*

My mother never accepted her move from Massachusetts and packed us children off every summer from our home in Michigan and took us "home." I do remember that my father seemed glad to watch us go. I still see him in our driveway with the parakeet in its cage, trying unsuccessfully to get my mother to take the bird too so that he wouldn't even have to be around to feed it. At the end of the summer, when we returned from Massachusetts, the bird would be there but it would never be the same bird. It was another $3.95 blue parakeet but without the gentleness of our old bird. When we reached into the cage to get our friend, we were usually bitten.

We traveled on one of the great lake boats that crossed Lake Erie to Buffalo and I remember the broad interior staircases and the brassbound window through which one viewed the terrific paddlewheels. I hoped intensely that a fish would be swept up from deep in the lake and brought to my view but it never happened. Then we took the train. I guess it must have been to Boston. I mostly remember my rapture as we swept through the eastern countryside over brooks and rivers that I knew were the watery world of the fish and turtles I cared so madly about. I also remember that one of these trips must have been made during hard times because my mother emphasized that there was enough money for us children to eat but not enough for her. We had wild highs and lows as my father tried to build a business.

Many wonderful things happened during my endless summers with my grandmother, aunts and uncles in Fall River; but for present purposes, I am only thinking of fishing. Those original images are still so burning that I cannot find a proper syntax for them. In the first, my father arrived and took me up to see some shirt-tail cousins in Townsend. A little brook passed through the backyard and, lying on my stomach, I could look into one of its pools and see the tiny brook trout swimming there. It was close to the rapture I felt when I held my ear against the slots of the toaster and heard a supernal music from heaven ringing the toaster springs. The brook trout were water angels and part of the first America, the one the Indians owned whose music I believed I heard from the springs of the toaster. I had seen the Indians' old trails, their burial mounds and the graves of settlers killed in the French and Indian wars. For some reason, I understood the brook trout had belonged to the paradise the Indians had struggled to keep.

It seemed to be part of a lost world like the world I was losing with my father as he became more absorbed in his work. It came to seem that we had good times together only when fish were present, and those brook trout are the first of those memories. It was casually easy for us to get along fishing; official father-and-sondom was a bomb. I think of the fathers and sons day at his athletic club with particular loathing, as it was an annual ordeal. Silver dollars were hurled into its swimming pool for the boys to struggle over. Each father stood by the pool, gazing at the writhing young divers, and waited for his silver-laden son to surface. I rarely came up with a coin. I was conscious of appearing to be less than an altogether hale boy and hardly worth bringing to this generational fête with its ventriloquists, Irish tenors, or more usually, the maniacal Eddie Peabody on the banjo. All of this was part of the background of the big dust we were meant to make in our mid-American boom town where sport of the most refined sort quickly sank into alcoholic mayhem. Steaks in the backyard, pill-popping housewives and golf were the order of the day and many youngsters sought to get their fathers away somewhere in search of a fish. Most of our fathers were just off the farm or out of small towns heading vertically upward into a new world. We didn't want them to go.

I thought that if I delivered a way to free my father from his rigorous job, we could fish more. I saw an ad for a Hart, Shaffner and Marx suit that said it was for the man who wanted to look like he would make $10,000 a year before he was thirty. Remember, this was many years ago. I told my father that he ought to make $10,000 a year, then $10,000 a year in eleven months, then $10,000 a year in ten months, and so on; and with this properly earned free time, he and I would go fishing together more often. My father said, "With an attitude like that, you'd never make $10,000 a year in the first place."

None of this mattered in Massachusetts. Across the street from my grandmother, across Brownell Street between Main and Almy, lived Jimmy McDermott, an elegant Irish bachelor who lived with his spinster sister, Alice, and they seemed very sophisticated and witty, especially compared to their immediate neighbors, the Sullivans, who were unreconstructed Irish, with a scowling mother in a black shawl and an impenetrable brogue. Jimmy McDermott took me fishing and bought me my first reel, a beautiful Penn Senator surf-casting reel, whose black density seemed to weigh coolly in my hands. Jimmy McDermott detected that I needed someone to take me fishing.

He thought it was crazy for a boy who loved to fish to be hanging around Brownell Street in Fall River in August; and so he packed a lunch and we went fishing for tautog along some small and lonely beach with its granite outcroppings and sunshot salty fog and tidal aromas. We caught several fish on the fierce green crabs we used for bait and I heard about several more because Jimmy was the sort of person who made sure at such a sacramental moment as angling that the full timbre of the thing must be appreciated in a recounting of holy incidents in time, of striped bass and flounders, of the gloomy conger eel who filled three skillets with grease,

ABOVE *A traditional thatched roof cottage at Boca Paila in the Yucatán. The locals particularly favor pastel shades for their homes.*

ABOVE *Poling smoothly and silently over white sand flats, as you stand ready in the bow, scanning and searching for the elusive quarry, is the ultimate test of patience and nerve.*

or the rich sports in the old days who baited their bass rigs with small lobsters. A Portuguese family picnicked on the nearby strand and in my somewhat more global view today, I think of us amusing ourselves on that *mare nostrum*, the Atlantic Ocean, casting our hopes on those ancestral waters toward Ireland, the Azores, toward the Old World. The sea heaved up around our rocks, pulling a white train of foam from mid-ocean and its mysteries of distance and language, drownings, caravels, thousand-foot unwitnessed thunderheads, phosphorous, and fish by the square mile.

LEFT *An assembly of permit flies. Modern crab patterns have evolved into many variations. Shown here are (left to right) the Brown Rattle Crab, the Swimming Crab; the Olive Turneffe Crab; the White Turneffe Crab; and the Beady Crab. A Clouser Minnow sits in front of them.*

It is a great triumph over something, biology maybe or that part of modern history which has prolonged adolescence to the threshold of senility, for a father to view his son without skepticism. I have not quite achieved this state but I have identified the problem. Therefore, when I stood at the airport in Cancún and watched my frequently carefree son emerge with several falling-apart carry-on bags and his shirt hanging out of his pants I did not take this altogether as a sign of complete disorganization. When we hugged, because he is so much stronger than I am, he rather knocked the wind out of me. And when we made our way to the small aircraft that would take us to Ascension Bay, I asked if he had practiced his casting. "Once," he said. "These aren't trout," I said, "a thirty-foot cast doesn't get it." "Don't worry about it," he smiled. "I don't expect to have any problem with bonefish." "How can you say that?" I asked. "You've never seen one before, you don't know how tough they can be." He just smiled. He knows how to drive me crazy.

We had a comfortable cottage, really wonderful, with cool concrete walls and a roof of thatched monkey palm. Birds were everywhere and the blue Caribbean breakers rose high enough that you could look right through them, then fell again. The coral garden seemed like a submerged quilt just past the line of breakers.

Thomas was slow getting ready to fish. He was bent over the sink, doing something and taking too long about it. I said we ought to hurry up and head for the boat. I said it twice. He straightened up from the sink holding a pale green scorpion he had just extracted from the drain. He said, "In case you were thinking of brushing your teeth." He grabbed his rod and we were out the door.

ABOVE *(following heads of flies clockwise from top) A Braided Cuda Fly; a Gray Clouser Minnow; a Rabbit Candy; two Chartreuse Clouser Minnows; and a Gaitorbraid Anchovy.*

ABOVE *A White Raghead Crab.*

Our guide was a Mayan Indian named Pedro, a solid fifty-year-old of easygoing authority. I thought of an Oak Bluffs voice of yesteryear, "We've been here for generations." Pedro's family had been on the shores of this bay since thousands of years before Christ. As Pedro was a mildly intolerant man, all business, one soon learned not to pester him with trifles. I did ask him if he had ever been to the United States.

ABOVE *A Chernobyl Crab.*

"I've never been to Mexico," he said coolly.

Walking to the boat, I was excited to see a lineated woodpecker who loves to eat Aztec ants from their home in the hollow pumpwood tree. A brave soul, he defends his nest against toucans. Ruddy ground doves scattered along our trail and we saw the splendid *chacalaca* on the edge of the jungle, noisy in flight as a chicken.

When we set out in the skiff, mangrove swallows scattered across the narrow channels. My son explained to me that some birds had taken to flying upside down over New York City because "there was nothing worth shitting on." Birds can tell us much.

Pedro ran the skiff through the shallow water wilderness with the air he seemed to bring to everything, an absence of ambiguity. There was no scanning the horizon, or search for signs. If a tremulous ridge of tidal movement betrayed a shoal in our path, Pedro adjusted his angle of travel without ever looking in the direction of the hazard.

When we emerged completely from the congestion of cays, the very similar bands of pale blue, of sky and sea, stretched before us at a sublime scale, white tropical clouds reaching upward to heavenly elevations. A scattering of small islands lay in the distance.

I was still thinking of Pedro's answer about never having been to Mexico. Quintana Roo was his country. In my minimal Spanish, I decided to pose a peculiar question to him. "Pedro, to us this is an extraordinary place, a beautiful place. But you have never been anywhere else. My question is this: Do you realize and appreciate that you live in one of the world's great places?"

Pedro pulled his head back and, pursing his lips to state the obvious, said in an impassioned growl, "*Sí, Señor!*"

Thomas was in the bow of the boat, line stripped out, and Pedro was poling along a muddy bank near the mangroves. A squadron of bonefish had come out of the light, our blind side, and flushed in a starburst of wakes. It wasn't really a shot; so, Thomas remained in the bow, ready. After a while, I felt Pedro kick the stern of the bow out to position him and declare, "*macabi*" – bonefish – in his quiet but insistent way that made it clear he expected no screw-ups. We stared hard, testing Pedro's patience, then made out the fish about seventy feet away. He was feeding slowly, his back out of water at times, and his tail glittering when he swirled deliberately in the shallows to feed. The fish came almost to a stop, faced right, then moved forward steadily but imperceptibly. The bonefish seemed to be staring at the skiff. This seemed like a tough prospect: the water was much too thin, the fish insufficiently occupied; and since the bonefish was alone, its green and silver shape all too clear, I couldn't imagine it would tolerate the slightest imperfection of technique.

ABOVE *A Rug Yarn Crab.*

ABOVE *A Nick's Casablanca Special.*

Thomas was false-casting hard. Faced with a good fish right in his face, his intensity was palpable throughout the boat. I told him that he was only going to get one shot at this fish, treading the parental thin-line of trying to remind him of the present cast. I watched his loop reach out straight, turn over, watched the fly fall about four inches in front of the bonefish.

The fish didn't spook. The fly sank to the bottom. Thomas moved the fly very slightly. The bonefish moved forward over it. I looked up and the bend of the rod extended all the way into the cork handle. The fish burned off through the mangrove shoots which bowed and sprang up obediently. When the fish headed out across the flat, Thomas turned to look at me over his shoulder and give me what I took to be a slightly superior grin. A short time later, he boated the fish.

We were actually fishing in the middle of the Sian Ka'an biosphere reserve – over a million acres of the coast of Quintana Roo, savannas, lagoons, seasonally flooded forest. Our camp, a simple comfortable place for fishermen called Casa Blanca, meets the Mexican requirement of integrating human use with preserving the complex and delicate local ecosystem whose uniqueness derives not only from the phenomenon of a tropic sea inundating a vast limestone shelf, but from long human history. Every walk that Thomas and I took brought us past the earth mounds that covered Mayan structures. One superb small temple has been excavated and its inspired siting caused us, hunched under its low ceilings, gazing out on the blue sea, with bones and pottery at our feet, to fall silent for a good while.

Since I have been unsuccessful in bringing any formality to the job of parenting, I wondered about the matter of generations, and whether or not the concept added much to the sense of cherished companionship I had with my son. And I thought of the vast timescape implied by our immediate situation and the words of the leader of the French Huguenots when the terrible Menéndez led his band of followers into a hollow in the dunes to slaughter them. "In the eyes of God," said the Huguenot, "what difference is twenty years, more or less?"

We wandered through the barracks of an abandoned copra plantation. A carved canoe paddle leaned against a wall, the kind of ancient design used to propel dugouts but probably a backup for the Evinrude. Inside, the walls were decorated with really splendid graffiti, ankle-grabbing stick ladies subjected to rear entry and the prodigious members of grinning stick hooligans with rakish brimmed hats and cigarettes. And there you have it.

My anxiety about whether or not Thomas would be able to handle bonefish disappeared. He did just fine. He is not as obsessive about fishing as I am; so, it was always a matter of harassing him to organize his tackle, be at the skiff on time, and to keep fishing instead of crawling around the mangroves to see what was living in there. We began to catch plenty of bonefish in a variety of situations: schooling fish in deep water, generally small, easy fish; small bunches lined up along the edge of a flat waiting for the tide to come and help them over. The singles and small

ABOVE *Sunsets in the Yucatán are wonderfully colorful and offer an opportunity to reflect on the day's activities.*

RIGHT *Moonrise over a beachside bungalow. Anglers on the porch celebrate the day with a tall, cold one.*

bunches, tailing and feeding, on the inside flats. Several times I looked up and saw Thomas at a distance, his rod deeply bowed and his fly line shearing an arc toward deeper water.

We were happy workers on a big bonefish farm.

"Pedro, are there many permit, *unas palomettas*?"

"Yes, of course."

"Have you had many caught in your skiff?"

"No one catches many *palomettas*."

"How many?"

"Maybe six this year."

169

Pedro stared in the direction he was poling, getting remarkable progress from the short hardwood crook he pushed us along with. Florida guides with their graphite eighteen-footers would refuse to leave the dock with an item like this one. He had a slightly superior look on his face, as though reading my thoughts. It was more likely that he felt the hopelessness of predictably catching a permit was his own secret. The look challenged you to try but declined to subdue skepticism.

After twenty-five years of pursuing permit, the intensity of the chase, the sense that the fish is an angler's Holy Grail, has never diminished. I feel, when searching for them, as a bird dog must when the unsearched country ahead turns into a binary universe of sign and absence of sign. Now I certainly couldn't expect my little son to feel the same way; here in the Sian Ka'an his attention was cast on all the wonders around us, the sea creatures scooting out in front of the skiff in response to Pedro's skillful poling, the spectacular flying squid that sailed across our bow, the cacophonous waterfowl that addressed our passage from the secrecy of the mangroves, the superb aerobatics of frigate birds trying to rob royal terns of their catch. Graciously, Thomas had offered me the first cast.

The little bay had a bottom too soft for wading. We were at a relatively low tide and the hermit crabs could be seen clinging to the exposed mangrove roots. A reddish egret made its way along the verge of thin water, head forward, legs back; then legs forward, head back until the sudden release, invisible in its speed, and the silver fish wriggles crossways in its bill.

Pedro said, "*Palometta*," and we looked back at him to see which way his phenomenal eyesight was directed. There was a school of permit coming onto the sandbar that edged the flat. Once noticed, the dark shape of the school seemed busy and its underwater presence was frequently enlarged by the piercing of the surface by the angular shapes of fins and tails. I checked to see if I was standing on my line. I tried to estimate again how much line I had stripped out. I held the crab fly by the hook between my left thumb and forefinger and checked the loop of line that would be my first false cast, now trailing alongside the boat. We were closing the distance fast and the permit were far clearer than they had been moments before. In fact, if they hadn't been so busy scouring around the bottom and competing with one another, they could have seen us right now.

The skiff ground to a halt in the sand. Pedro said that I was going to have to wade to these fish. Well, that was fine; but the only permit I have ever hooked

RIGHT *Over endless miles of poling and searching, the only sounds are the wind, and the occasional wave slapping on the hull of the boat. With talking kept to a minimum, sometimes the mind drifts, and it is then that the fish will usually come.*

wading spooled me while I stood and watched them go. Furthermore, I was using a Hardy freshwater reel, lots of backing but no drag. I picked it for the sporting enhancement it provided. This now seemed foolhardy.

I climbed out, eyes locked on the fish.

"Dad!" came Thomas' voice. "I've got to try for these fish too!"

"Thomas, God damn it, it's my shot!"

"Let me give it a try!"

"They're not going to take your bonefish fly anyway."

How could I concentrate? But now I was nearly in casting position. I heard something behind me. Thomas had bailed out of the boat. He was stripping line from his reel. He was defying his father! Our Mayan guide, Pedro, was celebrating his 3,000 years of family life on this bay by holding his sides and chuckling. For all I knew, he had suggested my son dive into the fray.

Once in casting range, I was able to make a decent presentation and the crab landed without disturbance in front of the school. They swam right over the top of it. They ignored it. Another cast, I moved the fly one good strip. They inspected it and refused. Another cast and a gingerly retrieve. One fish eased away from the school, tipped up on the fly and ate. I hooked him and he seared down the flat a short distance then shot back into the school. Now the whole school was running down the flat with my fish in the middle of it. Thomas waded to cut them off and began to false cast. I saw disaster staring at me as his loop turned over in front of the school and his fly dropped quietly.

RIGHT *A very happy angler with his first permit.*

"Got one!" he said amiably as his permit burned its way toward open water. Palming my whirling reel miserably, I realized why he had never been interested in a literary career. He wasn't sick enough to issue slim volumes from the interior dark. He was going to content himself with life itself. He seemed to enjoy the long runs his fish made; mine made me miserable.

Pedro netted Thomas' fish, his first permit, and waited with it, held underwater, until mine was landed. Thomas came over with the net. When the fish was close, I began to issue a stream of last-minute instructions about the correct landing of a permit. He just ignored them and scooped it up.

It was unbelievable, a doubleheader on fly-caught permit. I was stunned. We had to have a picture. I asked Pedro to look in my kit for the camera. Pedro admitted that he had only had this happen once before. He groped in my kit for the camera.

But I had forgotten the camera. Thomas saw my disappointment. He grabbed my shoulders. He was grinning at me. All my children grin at me as if I was crazy in a sort of amusing way. "Dad," he said, "it's a classic. Don't you get it?" He watched for it to sink in. "It's better without a picture." The permit swam away like they knew we weren't going to keep them anyway. Later, I stewed over his use of the word "classic." It was like when he buried a bonefish fly in the calf of my leg. He said that my expression was "timeless." I'd have to think about it.

LEFT *Early morning at Casa Blanca on Lighthouse Point. It's only a short walk from the cottage to the shore, so you can wander down with your morning coffee. Permit and coffee go together quite nicely – both set the blood racing!*

173

MEXICO – FACTFILE

BACKGROUND

The Caribbean coast of Mexico's Yucatán Peninsula may perhaps, for some, have unpleasant associations with the skyrise hotels of Cancún and Cozumel. However, over the last 10 years the Yucatán has become known as perhaps the world's most enjoyable of fly-tackle saltwater destinations. The diversity of the fishing and its healthy abundance has been nurtured by the United Nations which, in collaboration with the Mexican Government, created the Sian Ka'an biosphere. This biosphere has 1.3 million acres of tropical forest, savannah, mangrove swamps, flats, keys, springs, and a significant part of the second-largest barrier reef in the world. The biosphere's regulations restrict commercial angling and, combined with the catch and release policies of all the local lodges, ensure a fishing quality that should continue to improve for years to come.

WHEN TO GO

There is little doubt that the Yucatán Peninsula and its combined flats fisheries are more or less a year-round resource, but as is common with many other destinations, there are high and low points with regard to weather patterns. Most lodges close between July and October when hurricane risk is greatest. The most changeable weather in terms of rain and cloud is between November and January when the peninsula as a whole can be threatened by cold fronts moving down from the US. The peak fishing time is from February until July, when the sun warms the flats, ocean winds become seabreezes, and fish are on the flats in the highest concentrations. The numbers of large permit and tarpon are improved due to annual spawning migrations which make their way up the coast south to north during these months, making forays into the bays and flats along the coastline. Average temperatures are between 70°F (19°C) and 85°F (28°C), humidity levels can be high toward the end of summer, and light clothing is absolutely essential.

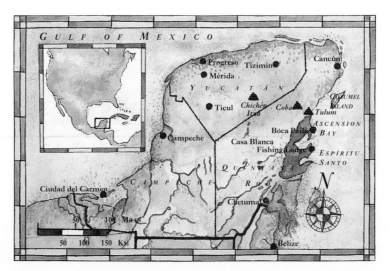

ANCIENT SITES

STATE BOUNDARY

NATIONAL BOUNDARY

SIAN KA'AN BIOSPHERE RESERVE

THE FISHING

Although the diversity of Mexico's Yucatán is well-known to all who've fished there, it is most often the numbers of bonefish and permit that have attracted anglers to its bay systems year after year. Resident fish abound on the flats, at times in great schools. In addition, tarpon and snook lurk under the shaded edges of mangrove lagoons. Mexico offers the best chance of the "Grand Slam" – a permit, a bonefish, and a tarpon all caught by one angler in a day. Whatever your preferred species may be, the geographical makeup of the lagoons and flats ensure an abundance of fly-fishing experiences.

If you decide to try for a permit, your guide will pole the endless flats, whether coral-bottomed or sandy, where the fish set up their feeding patrols.

Tarpon are usually found in the quieter, deeper, more sheltered mangrove lagoons, but occasionally giants on their migrational runs will be encountered in the shallow flats as they prospect into the bays. Nothing is guaranteed to make the heart beat faster in a fisherman than preparing himself and his tackle as the guide positions the skiff at an oncoming school of 100 lb tarpon.

It is the bonefish, though, that remains at the top of the quarry list of fish that are found on the flats. You may choose between being poled in a canoe or wading into the countless hard-bottomed flats, in search of individual bones or the huge schools of them that abound in these waters.

For anyone who has not experienced a bonefish searing off into the distance, after having stalked and successfully ambushed it on the flats, Mexico is a beginner's paradise. The large individual bonefish, which can weigh up to 10 lbs, provide excitement for the experienced angler, as do permit (notoriously fickle but powerful flats fish).

Although generally the tarpon here are not as large as those in Africa or the Florida Keys, they have been found weighing up to 150 lbs. Tarpon make up the last of the "big three" most commonly fished species in Mexico. Other species that can be caught on the fly include the aforementioned snook, barracuda (which are abundant, large, and under-rated), a multitude of snapper species, jacks, and small sharks.

TACKLE

RODS: Owing to the numbers of species likely to be encountered in a day, it is wise to have a cross-section of tackle, which will ensure that whatever fish you find, whether in a boat or wading, your rod is prepared and can be handed to you by your guide. Opportunities for a cast, especially at permit, may be fleeting, and an angler will not have time to change leaders and flies to suit a situation.

Nine feet is the ideal length to punch a line into the stiff breezes occasionally encountered, 10 to 12 wt for tarpon, 8 to 10 wt for permit, and 7 to 9 wt for bonefish. A useful fourth rod would be a 9 ft, 9 wt rod rigged with a wire tippet leader for barracuda and jacks.

REELS: Most fishermen opt for single-action reels with advanced adjustable drag systems that allow greater control of a runaway fish. All reels should hold the fly line plus a minimum of 150 yards of 30 lb braided Dacron backing.

LINES: Although there have been some experiments made with slow sinking lines and sinking-tips, nearly all fishermen use floating lines.

LEADERS: **Bonefish and permit** – 9 ft tapered leaders should be 8 to 15 lbs in strength, which will give you a little extra strength for bonefish in the more mangrove-filled flats. Don't think about using less than 12 lb for permit unless you've caught a few already or you're out to catch a specific IGFA line class record!

Tarpon and Snook – Buy or make tarpon leaders with a shock tippet of no less than 60 lbs and a class tippet strength of 16 lbs or more.

Barracuda – Use a 9 ft leader incorporating an 18 inch to 24 inch length of wire tippet with crimp system for easy changing of flies. The leader should be 15 lbs to 20 lbs strain with the wire tippet 25 to 40 lbs strength.

FLIES: Shrimps, small crustaceans, and baitfish make up the majority of food for all flats species. Practically all flats flies are imitations of these quarry species, though naturally there are favorites for different fish.

Tarpon – Sea-ducers, Cockroaches, Tarpon Bunnies, Whistlers, and Deceivers.

Permit – Rag-head Crab, McCrab, Isley Crab, Chernobyl Crab, Mother of Epoxy, and Clouser Minnow.

Bonefish – Crazy Charlie, Snapping Shrimp, Yucatán Special, Gotcha, Bonefish Bitters, and Gregs Flats Fly are all good examples, but there are also several other patterns.

Barracuda and Jacks – Poppers, Tarpon flies of all kinds, Needlefish patterns, and Oversize Clouser Minnows.

ESSENTIAL TRAVEL EQUIPMENT

Dress for Mexican flats fishing should consist of shorts and tee-shirts if you feel comfortable in the sun, with plenty of sunblock. In any situation, however, flats fishing exposes you to a lot of reflected sunlight, which can burn more than direct sunlight. There are several companies that manufacture long wading trousers and long-sleeved shirts made from quick-drying material. Bring a lightweight rain jacket for passing showers. Total block sun cream for the face, neck, and hands is great, but check that it won't damage your fly line or leader as some of them do. Sun creams with a protection fact of 15 to 30 are good for legs and arms. A good hat that offers shade for your eyes, ears, and neck is vital and will assist in spotting fish. Good polarized glasses are invaluable. Pliers, Hemostats, or long-nose pliers, for unhooking toothy predators like barracuda, are vital. A small knife, or clippers, is useful in cutting some of the thicker nylon used, especially shock tippets. A small pair of binoculars for looking at the many species of bird and mammal life that inhabit the flats and mangrove lagoons are a good idea if you can tear yourself away from the fishing. If you can't, then a camera for the one that didn't get away is a must, though make sure you have a sealable waterproof bag in which to house it.

FLIES: LEFT-HAND THREE Merkin Crabs.
MIDDLE THREE, TOP TO BOTTOM A Nick's Casablanca Special; a Chernobyl Crab; and an Olive Rag-head Crab.
RIGHT-HAND TWO, TOP TO BOTTOM A White Rag-head Crab and a Rug Yarn Crab.

ABOVE *The permit is one of the most difficult fish to fool with the fly. Catching one is considered to be a milestone in one's fishing career, and the Yucatán Peninsula is probably the best place to try for them. Their sickle-shaped fins and their big black eyes make them a very sensuous-looking fish.*

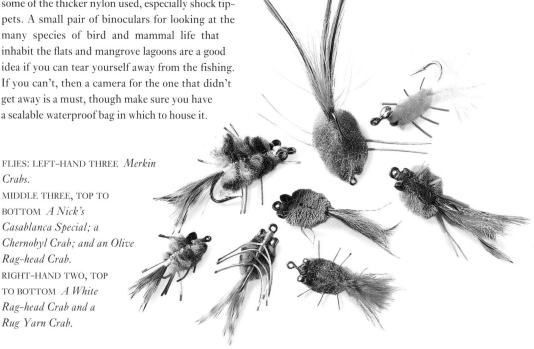

My Platform of Despair

Iceland

ART LEE

"Here the broad Laxá narrows dramatically, with churning rapids at the head, below which the pool plumps a bit and has dug deep enough into the lava bedrock bottom to provide good holding lies (although you might not think so to see the rush of water over the top), but just as quickly narrows again to pour with incredible power over a plate of lava no more than twenty feet wide, under a bridge and into a maelstrom of frothing white water below."

Among the many reasons Iceland's Laxá I Adaldal is my favorite Atlantic salmon river is that just as when you shoot ducks, you do well to hit. Five hundred in baseball – that is, land one-half of the salmon you hook. The greater your skill, the higher your average may turn out to be; but overall, year in and year out, that's more or less the way it goes. Make a mistake and your fish is gone. Isn't that the way salmon fishing really ought to be? You bet.

But what makes Laxá different than, say, New Brunswick's Miramichi or most Gaspé rivers, the "name" rivers of Scotland, or for that matter, the general run of Icelandic salmon rivers and streams? After all, at first glance Laxá isn't a brute by any means. In fact, though wide and carrying a lot of water, its spring creek appearance, reminiscent of Idaho's Henry's Fork, might even con you into thinking that landing Laxá salmon will be a piece of cake.

But there's the weed, for instance, especially late in the season. Ever try to control a twenty-pound salmon with ten pounds of weeds draped over the leader and line? No mean feat, believe me. And then there's all that submerged lava, always abrasive and sometimes as sharp as razor blades, and so tough as hell on leaders. Let a fish fool around near the bottom of most Laxá pools, and you're in big trouble, brother, to say the least.

There's also the size of the fish. Each year several salmon of thirty pounds and more are hooked on Laxá, not only on flies, but on bait and spoons, but precious few are landed. I've taken a pair of 29's and a few 28's, but only one of more than thirty pounds – a 33-pounder which, as I wrote elsewhere several years ago, is the only salmon I've ever caught to which I claim "braggin' rights." The small flies often necessary to attract Laxá salmon, even when the water is high, are also a crucial factor. Sizes six to fourteen are usually more effective than larger flies. Liphook a fifteen-pounder on a size twelve Hairy Mary Orange, then permit a gob of weed to slide down the leader against the hook, and you're done like a dinner.

An unforgiving river is this Laxá I Adaldal, and that's why, at least in part, in a country of so many "Laxás," this one warrants its special designation "the Laxá."

As far as I know, I'm the only American who has fished every salmon pool on the river, and I hope no one will find it unduly immodest when I say that over the years I've given as good as I've got. Except on one pool: Núpafossbrún, which has been "kickin' my ass" for more than twenty years. This is the one place on Laxá where, as the late hotelier-sportsman Charles Ritz lamented of his misadventures with the always colorful Count Denissoff on the Russian exile's Åaro and its

RIGHT *The blue boat on upper beat number three, moored in the wet grass, allows anglers to fish the deeper parts of the pool, which can't be reached from the shore. The boat waits there year after year in exactly the same spot. Some things never change.*

ABOVE *A traditional sheepskin fly wallet shows off a variety of Icelandic flies, both single hook and double. An old saying, "bright day, bright fly; dark day, dark fly," helps with selection.*

"Platforms of Despair," I have been "pursued by continuous bad luck."

For sheer power, Núpafossbrún, interestingly enough, is the one pool on Laxá which might contend with the tumultuous Åaro and its famed (or infamous) "Platforms." Since most Americans who fish Laxá know the pool only as "the bridge at [beat] number seven," it may not matter, but for the record, translated from the Icelandic, Núpafossbrún means "brink of the falls beneath a steep hill," with the Núpa complicating things a bit, being the dative case of an old Icelandic word (*núpur*) which also situates the pool on the farmstead to which it belongs.

Here the broad Laxá narrows dramatically, with churning rapids at the head, below which the pool plumps a bit and has dug deep enough into the lava bedrock bottom to provide good holding lies (although you might not think so to see the rush of water over the top), but just as quickly narrows again to pour with incredible power over a plate of lava no more than twenty feet wide, under a bridge and into a maelstrom of frothing white water below. So powerful is this compacted flow, in fact, were it not for a tight, but deep, crevasse, left by nature in the lava plate near the east bank, I doubt that any salmon, even salmon as powerful as those for which Laxá is famous, could ascend this foss.

As luck would have it, Núpafossbrún isn't at all difficult to fish from the west

179

side, or low side of the river, except that relatively few salmon tend to lie to that side of a potent whitewater current which more or less bisects the pool. And while it's also easy enough for a skillful angler to cast most of the way across the meat of the pool, that midstream surge causes your flies to bolt so quickly from east to west that it's unlikely many salmon in the prime lies even see the flies, much less are inclined to chase them. So, for your best shot at Núpafossbrún salmon, you have no choice but to fish from three flat-topped *hraunpallar*, or "platforms" of lava which are part of the *höfði*, or bluff, which, in turn, is part of that *núpur*, or hill of grass, rock and blueberry bushes which rises steeply several hundred feet behind you on the east side of the pool. Or to fish *klöppunum*, that is, "from the cliffs," as some Icelanders like to put it, which loom over Núpafossbrún's real hotspots.

Now, except for the fact that you have to cast about as much up-and-down as sideways just to reach the water, to fish Núpafossbrún effectively – unless maybe you're a severe acrophobe – is probably not as difficult as mastering enough of the Icelandic language to describe the setting at all colorfully and make yourself read smartly. You can't see them, even from such height, but the salmon are always lying right there in front of you, and unless you try to cast too far, which would defeat your purpose for fishing from there in the first place, there's plenty of room between the *hraunpallar* and the *núpur* for a backcast.

Picture yourself standing high over this water, tight to a salmon and knowing that should that salmon decide to leave the pool, either it's gone, simple as that, or you're in for the adventure of your lifetime when you try to scramble down the rocks and under the bridge on a narrow catwalk immediately adjacent to the reality of death in the form of furious water and potentially murderous boulders. That will give you some idea of why taking a fish at Núpafossbrún has to be Laxá's ultimate thrill and crowning achievement, not for the awkward afoot or faint of heart.

And given this, you can probably also understand why I'm so goddamned frustrated by the fact that virtually everyone with whom I've fished Núpafossbrún over the last quarter century – from my first Laxá fishing partner, the late Dave Danzig, back in 1972, to my present fishing partner, Galen Mercer, just a couple of years ago – has tasted that experience. Everyone, that is, except yours truly.

Hell, Dave took a pair of 22-pound males in one week, both perfect "gentlemen" who fought the good fight but never even threatened to depart the premises, while Galen hooked and landed a nice sixteen-pound cock the very first time he ever laid eyes on the spot. Then, to add insult to injury, I began raising a good

ABOVE *Pétur Steingrímsson, a famous Icelandic guide, shares a few of his secrets with a visiting fisherman. He often "wears" his favorite patterns.*

Núpafossbrún salmon just seconds after Galen's fish was safely in guide Volundur Hermodsson's net, a salmon that "looked" eight times at an array of flies without taking before I finally had to call it a night (notwithstanding all onlookers kindly ignoring their wristwatches), since the blinkin' fish was still teasing me a full fifteen minutes after Iceland's statutory 10 pm quitting time. Even when desperate, you can only stretch the rules so far.

But I'm a confident salmon fisherman in the main and have always believed, despite a superstitious streak rooted no doubt either in the sod of Ireland or the clans which fought the border wars between England and Scotland, or both, that one day I'd hook my Núpafossbrún salmon while "standin' tall" on one of those *hraunpallar* high over the pool, and that my fish would be a "whopper." I blush to think how many times I've envisioned the perfect take, the ensuing battle of such epic proportions, including, of course, the risk of life and limb, as to one day prompt some brooding Icelandic poet on a dark winter day to pen the Artúr Núpafossbrún Saga which would forever after take its leatherbound place alongside the Njálssaga, the most famous of them all, the Gisla saga Súrssonar, on which a nifty period flick called *The Outlaw* was made, and the forty-odd other sagas for which this island nation of Viking heirs is renowned.

However, dreams are dreams and reality is reality, and so it was when I found myself faced with Núpafossbrún once again last August, I allowed my soul to slip from the former place to the latter, something a salmon fisherman should never, never do, at least not entirely. In other words, I took to the *hraunpallar* with more emphasis on the exercise of memory of past failures than on the exercise of hope, and aren't "the infinite opportunities to exercise hope," after all, as John Buchan reminded us so brilliantly, why we're really doing it in the first place?

I had two rigged rods in the rod racks on the car roof: one a fourteen-footer for a number ten line and a 2.5-to-1 multiplying reel with the most potent drag I've ever used; the second, a rod of the same length but for a number nine line and carrying a reel with a basic, though certainly sound, pawl drag. Riding in the car, I had already asked Galen to permit me first shot at the *hraunpallar* side of Núpafossbrún and had decided to tackle it with the stouter stuff for obvious reasons. But something also told me that I wanted to fish a Stardust fly, a pattern of my own design, the one on which I'd taken the 33-pounder from Laxá several years earlier. At this point, I'd have to guess now, my soul was still more or less in trim.

But then upon alighting from the car, I looked up at the roof and what fly pattern do you suppose was already cinched pretty as you please to the lighter

BELOW *A Garry Dog.*

outfit? Yup, a Stardust, a new one sparkling in a shaft of sunshine that burst through a hole in the clouds of this generally overcast afternoon. How distinctly I remember looking at the fly which seemed to sing in the bright light, then at both rods and knowing what I ought to do. But instead of taking the, what, one minute necessary to transfer the Stardust from one tippet to the other, I opted to utter the unforgivable, "Might as well grab the light rod, Steini [Steini Stefansson, my guide]. You and I both know I never catch any salmon here anyhow."

Galen and I may have discussed the what-iffiness of my decision for a moment. I don't recall now. What I do know is that there was no Sibyl present, either within or without me, to remind me as Virgil wrote in *The Aeneid*: "Easy is the descent to hell . . . but to return, to regain the outer air, now that is the rub, that is the task."

And so I crossed the narrow bridge over the torrent at the tailout of Núpafossbrún with light rod and pawl reel at shoulder arms, probably humming a Sinatra tune. Oblivious.

ABOVE *The boat pool on lower beat number one bathes in hillside reflections on a quiet summer evening.*

183

Reaching the first *hraunpallar*, the favorite lava platform of Icelandic wormers, the water looked black as always beneath me and wildly white at midstream. I stripped just enough line off the reel to reach the water perhaps fifteen feet below and began fishing much as one would do when covering any salmon pool with a wet fly – short to long – until after ten or so arm-length pulls of line, my Stardust was landing all the way out in the heavy current, then sweeping smoothly inboard towards me. Nothing showed and so I reeled in and picked my way along the precarious dirt path between the rocks to *hraunpallar* number two, the platform from which every angler in the universe, it seemed to me, had hooked a Núpafossbrún salmon but me.

Again, I stripped the five or six pulls of line needed to reach Laxá's surface, and once again began extending one pull per cast after the fly had swept the water to the base of the lava *höfði*, the bluff. From high over the water I could clearly see the fly, its dark silhouette planing just below the surface.

Whether it was on line-pull number four or number five that she came, I cannot tell you now for sure. But I can tell you that it was on a very short line and that I could see her clearly, polished silver rising out of the pitch to inhale my swinging fly. So close that I could also see that she was a she not a he, that she weighed at least 25 pounds, and that she was as fresh from the sea as fresh could be. So close that even as I tightened on her, I had that first inkling, born of fighting more salmon than it might be seemly to say, that I was in big trouble as the result of having made a big mistake. In fact, perhaps the best way to sum up my position, even as early as this moment, lies in guide Steini's concise assessment: "Oh shit."

Now before proceeding to center ring, much less into the clinches or against the ropes, there are a few things you ought to know about the August salmon of Laxá I Adaldal in general and those which hold in Núpafossbrún in particular.

First, is that most of big Laxá's females arrive early, or from late June through mid-July. A fresh August female is real rarity, not to mention a real prize. Second, is that Laxá hens exceeding twenty pounds are also relatively uncommon, regardless of the period. Third, most of the Laxá's largest salmon are males which, for whatever reason, whether they're fresh or not, simply don't fight nearly as hard as the river's females. Or put another way, to play a twenty-plus pound Laxá female is arguably comparable to doing battle with a fresh forty-pounder on most great salmon rivers, no mean feat, even when optimally tackled.

That's the "downside." The "upside" is that gaining entrance to Núpafossbrún is so hard-earned for any salmon that once in the pool, most are

FAR LEFT *One afternoon I tore myself away from the fishing and climbed into the hills for a bird's-eye view of the spectacular surrounding countryside.*

BELOW *A discussion of tackle and technique draws a curious crowd. The pool in the background is that described by Art Lee in the essay. The falls drop away under the bridge.*

LEFT *A Rusty Rat.*

RIGHT *A Silver Doctor.*

disinclined to leave it, even in the heat of battle. Time and again, I've seen fish tear right to the brink, only to suddenly reverse course as if to say: "Even getting caught is better than going through that again." And so if your salmon is small enough to be easily handled or a typical fish, though big perhaps, you have a reasonable chance of ultimately seeing it in the net.

Given a big, fresh female fish, however, all bets are off, a reality I recognized only too well from the outset.

The early rounds of this fight were at once promising and sobering in that, after a few head shakes characteristic of most salmon after the take, the fish ripped off across the river and upstream, rather than down – indicating on the one hand she might hang around, while on the other, instantly underscoring my blunder back at the car, as my pawl reel, drag-tightened to the max – was literally shrieking, even as I burned my fingertips while trying desperately to slow her down a little by creating additional break.

What is more, though I was stationed over the water, she had already managed to bury my line, which became acutely evident when, high in the pool, she leapt through the foam – a glorious sight – then turned and tore downstream again to a point not far from that at which she had taken the fly. Me? At that moment my total preoccupation was trying desperately to get back some line.

Planted as I was atop a *hraunpallar*, I had nowhere to go, after all, not as you do when you're playing big fish under "normal" circumstances, say from a gravel beach or grassy bank. Certainly no putting the rod over your shoulder and walking upstream, your fish following like an obedient pooch. All I could do was to hold on and think, use rod pitch and angles and adjustments of hook pressure points in hopes of convincing her that what I wanted, no, *needed* her to do – to stay abreast or above me – also represented her best chance of escape.

But talk about chancy. Which way do you go? Do you angle your rod to the left, that is, upstream, for instance, fancying that she'll take the hint; or go for broke and angle it downstream, or toward the tail of the pool and

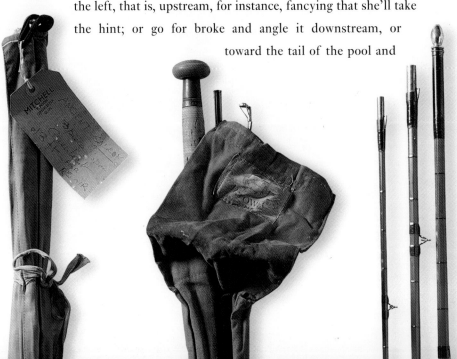

the maelstrom below, praying she'll believe you want her to go that way and so play into your hands by doing the opposite?

I opted for the former, but it made no difference, as she went neither up nor down, but instead raced directly across the pool where she made two more stunning jumps before once more allowing me to pump and reel her back almost to the point at which we'd first met.

And then she did what I guess I somehow knew she would do from the very outset. Side-on to me, she began to edge away, until at about midstream, she turned slowly inboard, that is, toward me, then suddenly bolted downstream for the tail of the pool. There, after only the briefest hesitation during which time she turned again to face upstream deep in the hole just ahead of the crevasse up through which she had no doubt swum into Núpafossbrún perhaps as recently as that very day, she turned once more and rushed down the shoot into the churning white water below. I can only wish now that you could have heard my reel beg for mercy as fly line and backing melted away, seemingly heading for sea faster that you'd want to drive a car on a good lava road.

I hope I wasn't born on the back of the train, and so by the time Steini and Galen were at my side, I had already struggled my way down the rocks to a point no more than five or six feet from the water raging over the lava plate, even as

BELOW *This is the moment of truth and high anxiety. Can the angler apply enough pressure to draw the fish into the net without breaking the leader?*

backing continued to seethe from my reel. There was no sign of fly line at all anymore. But it's funny, isn't it, how your mind can focus on two things at once without drifting, even in a crisis? And so whereas I was confident I could get the fish if I could just make it under that bridge, I was struck by a vivid memory of my longtime Icelandic friend Ingvi Jónsson, or Ingvi Rafn ("Black Raven") as we still call him, wending his way under the bridge with great difficulty when we were both 25 years younger and considerably less copious at the midriff.

"I've got to try to follow her," I told Galen nonetheless.

"You can't," Galen shouted over the roar of the foss. "The catwalk is too narrow, and if you go in, you could be done for. I'm not sure I could do it." Galen is twenty years younger than me and agile as a cat.

"I've got Steini," I shouted. Steini, a nickname related to the Icelandic word *steinn*, or stone, fits the moniker perfectly. In his late twenties, he looks like an NFL Pro-Bowl guard and is well known as the "bouncer" upon whom the local police rely to bail them out when they get into trouble trying to handle the worst offenders among huge crowds of boozing young people drawn from miles around to local dances. "He can hang onto me."

"And you'll probably both go in. Steini's strong, but he's no ballet dancer," Galen said just loud enough for me to hear. But his jaw was set. "If you want, I'll take the rod and try to go under, but you, no way."

ABOVE *This happy angler proudly displays his first Laxá salmon – a memorable moment.*

All anglers, it would be hoped, have certain quasi-religious principles, and one of mine is, "Thou shalt never pass a rod." Whether bluegill or blue marlin, if it's not one-on-one, it isn't sport. To pass a rod disgraces both fisherman and fish. But on the other hand, I had never lost a fly line to a fish of any species or size and this, too, had taken on some religious significance over the years. So perhaps you can sympathize with my quandary, as staring downstream, the only fish on earth that mattered a whit to me at that moment was adding insult to injury by taking her Nemesis' colors as she widened the distance between us. But the most depressing part of all was the realization that Galen had been absolutely correct – that for the first time in my long career astream, there was something truly beyond me, something I could no longer do and be sure of living to scribble the tale for you to read later.

Meantime I had not even noticed my reel's sudden silence, and as I glanced down the bank at the very brink of the shoot, there was Steini, my backing in hand, pulling it toward him hand over hand with all his strength. "It does not matter," he called back over his shoulder with the look of the greatest kindness and deepest

sympathy I have ever witnessed on the face of a guide. "The fish did cut off on the rocks down there and has been gone for a long time. Shit."

"I wonder how often Denissoff felt like I do when he owned the Åaro 'Platforms'?" I muttered to no one in particular as the three of us crossed the bridge on our way back to the car. Beneath us the funneled-down Laxá continued to rage toward a broad and gentle pool not far downstream.

"Sometimes, but for him, there was always tomorrow," Galen answered over Laxá's roar, and Steini nodded, although it's unlikely the young Icelander had ever heard of the onetime finance minister to Russia's last Czar, or the salmon of the short but mighty Norwegian river which had tested his will and tortured his tackle until the day he died.

ABOVE *Guide Pétur Steingrímsson and visiting angler Bill Young share a moment of camaraderie on the walk back to the lodge. It's been a good day.*

ICELAND - FACTFILE

BACKGROUND

Iceland, which lies midway between Greenland and Norway, is appropriately named the "Land of Ice and Fire." A place of extreme contrasts and few trees, Iceland is enormously mountainous, with high snow-covered peaks, glaciers, and active volcanoes. The country is still being transformed by the constant forces of nature.

There are at least 50 salmon rivers in Iceland, the best of them mostly on the north and west coasts, with a few to the south. Usually the rivers are fast and rocky with numerous waterfalls and rapids. Some rivers are clean, others have the typical milky coloration of glacier-fed streams. The salmon are not large, but they are numerous, averaging between 5 and 15 lbs, with occasional fish between 20 and 30 lbs.

The Laxá I Adaldal, featured in this chapter, is considered to be one of the very finest salmon rivers in all of Iceland. Located near the northern village of Húsavík, it has the largest average size fish of any river in the country. Its source is Lake Mývatn, the fourth-largest lake in Iceland, which is surrounded by volcanic craters and hot springs. From here the Laxá flows northward to the Greenland Sea.

WHEN TO GO

The fishing takes place during the short Icelandic summer, which in these extreme northern latitudes may last for only 3 months. The best weeks are in July and August. The climate on the island is actually milder than the name "Iceland" suggests. The Gulf Stream brings a temperate climate, with summertime temperatures averaging in the 50's.

Rainfall is lower in the northern part of the island at approximately 16 inches per year, compared with up to 160 inches of rain on the southern slopes. The mean temperature in the north is approximately 29°F (-2°C) in January, rising to approximately 52°F (11°C) in July. First-time Atlantic salmon anglers should understand and accept the unpredictability of conditions. Even during the best fishing weeks, weather and water temperatures – not to mention angling ability – can halve or double a catch.

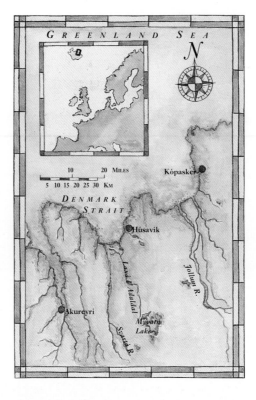

THE FISHING

A fighting Atlantic salmon will invariably thrill you, usually with a visible surface take and often with long runs and jumps that result in a hugely spectacular battle.

An angler should move slowly and methodically through the holding water – one of the most common mistakes is staying riveted too long in one spot. Begin with short casts, lengthening each one to your comfortable capacity, then move a couple of feet downstream with every few casts. Sometimes the salmon will show his back or tail, or push a wave of water toward your fly when he is coming after it. It takes discipline and control not to pull the fly away from him at this time, before he has had a chance actually to take. As a general rule, wait until you feel the fish and then lift your rod in a firm, deliberate manner to hook him. Work patiently on any fish that shows interest in your fly without taking it. Try him with different patterns, rest him awhile, and then go after him again. Once a fish shows, it generally means interest, and if he doesn't take the fly the first time he may come again.

Check your hook points frequently as Iceland's rivers are very rocky and hooks tend to break if they hit rocks on the back-cast.

Most Atlantic salmon-fishing in Iceland is done with a floating line and predictable fly patterns on known holding lies. Icelandic fish are very energetic. Their inherited genetic makeup has built them to negotiate fast water and jump high falls. They are more streamlined than most species of Atlantic salmon, with small heads, and fat bodies – a crowning challenge and achievement on a fly rod.

THE TACKLE

RODS: Graphite rods, both single- and double-handed models, are popular in Iceland. Single-handed rods in lengths of 9 ft to 10 ft are preferred for line weights 7 to 10. Double-handed rods are popular in lengths of 12 to 15 ft for line weights 9 to 12. Most of your fishing will not require casts of more than 60 ft.

However, there are pools and runs that do require long casts, and here the double-handed rod comes into its own. You can cover more water, more efficiently with a double-hander. You will need rods that can cast well in the windy conditions common in Iceland. Multi-piece travel rods are ideal, as these break down into smaller pieces and are carried directly onto the plane for safe keeping.

REELS: Any good-quality, single-action fly reel that will hold the correct weight line plus at least a 100 yards of backing will do the job. You can control drag fairly accurately by exerting finger pressure on the outside of the spool. Nevertheless, many anglers prefer higher-precision reels with sophisticated drag systems.

LINES: Most of the fishing in Iceland's waters is with a weight-forward floating line. On an extra spool, it might be useful to take a sinking-tip line, which can be used to fish the deeper sections of the pools or during high-water conditions.

LEADERS: Leaders of 9 ft tapered down to a tippet strength of 10 to 15 lbs are usually sufficient on most Icelandic rivers. On the whole, Atlantic salmon are not leader-shy.

FLIES: There are many theories about fly selection for salmon fishing. The following is one of the most popular: "A dark pattern is chosen when salmon see it against low, shaded sun; a medium-colored pattern when the sun is high or not shining; and a light or bright one for flash when the sun is behind the salmon." In *Fishing Atlantic Salmon Flies* (Stackpole Books, 1996) by Joseph Bates, Jr. and Pamela Bates-Richard, Colonel Bates wrote that the most popular fly in Iceland, and the one fly that represents over half of all salmon flies sold in Iceland, is the Red Francis originated by the famous British fly tyer, Peter Drake.

Other recommended patterns are: Black Doctor, Hair-wing March Brown, Crossfield, Blue Charm, Night Hawk, Green Butt, Collie Dog, Munroe Killer, Undertaker, Laxa Blue, Black Sheep, and Ally's Shrimp. Size 6 flies should be considered the average size to use. Many Icelandic anglers believe that the double-hook fly swims a bit deeper and is a bit more stable in the water. Some prefer to use single-hook patterns if they encounter weeds or low water. These flies are also essential in the "riffled hitch" method of fishing Atlantic salmon, so popular in Iceland. Dry fly patterns can also be used but, generally speaking, Iceland is noted as a small pattern destination. Tube flies tend to work better early in the season.

ESSENTIAL TRAVEL EQUIPMENT

As the weather can be extreme in Iceland, neoprenes are recommended for warmth. The layered approach to dressing is wise. You can put on or take off layers to maintain a comfortable body temperature. Fleece or capilene underwear works well to keep you warm and keeps perspiration or moisture from your body as you become active. A high-quality rain and wind jacket, along with a rain hat and fingerless gloves, are a must. Polarized sunglasses (with UV protection) and a travel alarm clock are important items, too. A camera and lots of film can go in a regular fishing vest along with the other things that you might usually carry with you.

FLIES: FAR RIGHT *A Silver Star.*
CLOCKWISE FROM TOP CENTER *A Teal-and-Blue Tube; a Micro Stoat's Tail Tube; a Hairy Mary; a Sweep; a Red Francis; a Willie Gunn; a Black Francis Tube; a Shrimp; a Collie Dog;, and a Black Stoat's Tail.*

ABOVE *Atlantic salmon, such as this one caught in Iceland, are often known as the "leapers" or "kings" of the gamefish. At one time, the Romans fished for this species. Over the centuries these kings have been pursued by nets and pitchforks, rods and reels. They grow very large and taste very good, but today's sportsmen recognize the value of this diminishing species, and more and more Atlantic salmon anglers are now stringently practicing policies of catch and release in order to preserve this beautiful quarry for generations to come.*

Acknowledgments

The publishers would like to thank the following authors and publishing houses/magazines for their kind permission to reproduce pieces in *Distant Waters*.

"Dances With Trout" John Gierach, an extract previously published in *Dances With Trout* (Simon and Schuster, New York, 1994).
Text copyright © John Gierach, 1994.

"Sterling Silver" Russell Chatham, previously published in *Silent Seasons: 21 Fishing Adventures by 7 American Experts* (E. P. Dutton, New York, 1978).
Text copyright © Russell Chatham, 1978.

"The Chalkstream Idyll" Neil Patterson, previously published in *The Chalkstream Chronicle: Living out the Flyfisher's Fantasy* (Merlin Unwin Books, London, 1995; Lyons and Burford, New York, 1995).
Text copyright © Neil Patterson, 1995.

"A Night at the Black Falls" Mike Fitzgerald.
Text copyright © Mike Fitzgerald, 1997.

"La Fiebre de las Bocas" Ernest Schwiebert, previously published in *Remembrances of Rivers Past* (The Macmillan Company, New York, 1972; Collier-Macmillan Limited, London, 1972).
Text copyright © Ernest Schwiebert, 1972.

"Mornings" Nick Lyons, previously published in *Spring Creek* (Atlantic Monthly Press, New York, 1992).
Text copyright © Nick Lyons, 1992.

"The Miramichi River" Leonard M. Wright, Jr.
Text copyright © Leonard M. Wright, Jr.

"Trout Among the Shadows" Verlyn Klinkenborg, previously published as "Trout Among the Kiwis" in *Esquire Magazine* (October 1988).
Text copyright © Verlyn Klinkenborg, 1988.

"Jingle Bones" Peter Kaminsky, previously published in *Field and Stream Magazine* (December 1985).
Text copyright © Peter Kaminsky, 1985.

"Fly-fishing in the Middle Ages" David Profumo.
Text copyright © David Profumo, 1997.

"Sons" Tom McGuane, previously published in *Live Water* (Meadow Run Press, New Jersey, 1996).
Text copyright © Thomas McGuane, 1996.

"My Platform of Despair" Art Lee, previously published in *Wild Steelhead and Salmon Magazine*.
Text copyright © Art Lee, 1997.

The publishers have made every effort to contact copyright holders. We should like to apologize for any errors or omissions, which we will endeavor to rectify in any future editions of this book.

Duncan Baird Publishers would like to thank Lord Stratford and the Piscatorial Society, Dru Montagu, the Laverstoke estate, and Janice Mitchell for allowing us to fish on and photograph their waters. We should also like to thank Farlow's of Pall Mall for their assistance.